THE VAMPIRE TRILOGY

David Pinner

THE VAMPIRE TRILOGY

FANGHORN

EDRED, THE VAMPYRE

LUCIFER'S FAIR

OBERON BOOKS
LONDON

This collection first published in 2011 by Oberon Books Ltd
521 Caledonian Road, London N7 9RH
Tel: 020 7607 3637 / Fax: 020 7607 3629
e-mail: info@oberonbooks.com
www.oberonbooks.com

A catalogue record for this book is available from the British
Library.

ISBN: 978-1-84943-088-3

Cover photography and design by James Illman

Contents

Preface

My fascination with vampires began as a schoolboy, when Christopher Lee terrified me as Dracula in the first famous Hammer Film. At the time little did I realise that seventeen years later, Christopher Lee would co-star with Edward Woodward in the cult movie, *The Wickerman,* which was based on my first novel, *Ritual.* I wrote *Ritual* when I was twenty-seven while I was playing the leading role of Sergeant Trotter in Agatha Christie's *The Mousetrap* at the Ambassadors Theatre. Although there are no actual vampires in my novel, it is redolent with occult predators and revenants.

The year before I wrote *Ritual,* I completed my fantasy comedy, *Fanghorn,* featuring a lesbian vampire. *Fanghorn* was one of the last plays to be banned by the Lord Chamberlain, so it couldn't be performed in London until the Chamberlain's Office was abolished. In 1967, Glenda Jackson played Tamara Fanghorn, Heir to the Winter of Drachfells, at the Fortune Theatre. As I wanted to satirise the then-current theatrical obsession with Antonin Artaud and his 'Theatre of Cruelty', I set the play in the gothic house of Joseph King, who may – or may not be – the First Secretary to the Minister of Defence. I filled King's kinky study by the sea, with rapiers, sabres, bullwhips and black candles. In the midst of this perverse armoury, the lesbian vampire, Fanghorn, appears as a stunning apparition in black leather. At the end of Act Two, in a grotesque Satanic Mass, she performs a ritual of emasculation, with the apparent approval of both Joseph's wife and his daughter. Allen Wright, the critic on *The Scotsman,* wrote at the time; 'If Henrik Ibsen, Jean Genet and Agatha Christie had collaborated on the script of *The Avengers,* they might have come up with something like *Fanghorn'.* It was my intention to turn everything on its head, so vampires, witchcraft, murdered bodies in the lettuce patch, and Grandpa, who is always so voraciously hungry that he eats the cheese out of every mouse-trap, are all seen as being an acceptable part of everyday life. In this surrealistic world, normality is perceived as perversion, and the dead are often more alive than the living, which is why I called *Fanghorn* a purple comedy.

Ten years later, in 1977, when I was the Writer-in-Residence for the Unicorn Theatre, I was commissioned by the Artistic Director, Matyelok Gibbs, to write a Hallowe'en play for children with songs. I based the twelve-year-old heroine, Honor, on my own daughter, who was the same age. The thirteen-year-old hero, Clive Sobers, I named 'Clive' after Clive Lloyd, and 'Sobers' after Gary Sobers because of my love of cricket. In order to scare my young audience as well as making them laugh, I set *Lucifer's Fair* in a fairground that is adjacent to a run-down cemetery. The play exposes the unreliability of grown-ups, so at the fair the children meet Winny, who is a hockey-stick teacher during the day, but at night she turns into the frightful Winny the Witch. Winny is aided by Fangs, the bovver boy, who, at twilight, transmogrifies himself into Fangs, the fearsome Vampire. The fair is owned by the crooked business magnate, Sir Lucifer Tombs. But when night falls, Lucifer becomes the Devil incarnate, and Lucifer turns the local policeman into Bruno the baleful Bear. But after numerous scarily-hilarious incidents, with the chaotic help of Miss E. Blyton, who is a totally-incompetent private-eye, at dawn the children vanquish all the forces of evil, and naturally they save the world.

33 years later, in 2010, I returned to writing about the world of the undead. Although there have been numerous novels, and films on TV and in the cinema on the subject, there have been very few stage plays on vampires. So I decided to create a thousand-year-old English, bi-sexual vampire, who slept with Shakespeare but never bit him. But I wanted my revenant to have an ancient, vampiric-sounding name, and in the Anglo Saxon Chronicles, I was delighted to find King Edred, who had a serious eating-disorder. Edred could only suck the blood out of meat, and I took this as a sign that I could transmogrify him into Edred the Vampyre. As I wanted my revenant to disprove all Bram Stoker's theories about how to kill the Undead, including their supposed fear of holy ground, I set my play in a village church, which Edred uses as his local pub. He keeps his wine behind the altar, and he tells the two students who track him down, via Google and Wikipedia, that 'my vino is far superior to the stuff the Vicar serves up'. Also Edred loves sunlight – 'which is the only thing that warms my old bones. And I developed my

penchant for garlic, when I dined on countless Moslems during the Crusades. As a result, ever since, Christians have always tasted rather bland.' Edred has lived through a thousand years of world history – which I explore in the play with the help of his two student intruders. But the play is also filled with mystery, suspense and insidious menace, and there is a startling revelation at the end of the play.

David Pinner, March 2011

FANGHORN

A COMEDY

Characters

JOSEPH KING
First Secretary to the Minister of Defence

JANE KING
Joseph's wife

JACKIE KING
Joseph's daughter

GRANDPA
Jane's father

TAMARA FANGHORN

WOLFY
a pussy-dog

HUMPH
a toy Panda

Fanghorn was first performed at the Fortune Theatre, Russell Street, London, WC2 on November 16th, 1967, produced by Michael Codron and Michael White, with the following cast:

JOSEPH KING, Peter Bayliss
JANE KING, Rachel Herbert
JACKIE KING, Mary Land
GRANDPA, Sydney Bromley
TAMARA FANGHORN, Glenda Jackson

Director, Charles Marowitz
Designer, Philip Prowse
Lighting, Francis Reid

ACT ONE

SCENE ONE

Late afternoon. August. 1966.

Hove, near Brighton.

JOSEPH KING's study is decorated in off-white. The room is in the shape of half of an ellipse. A vast curved window dominates the study, and looks out onto the sea. There are curved French doors in the centre of the window, and two carpeted steps lead up to the doors. Either side of the window are two large doors. Stage Left door leads to a passageway and the garden, while Stage Right door leads to the stairs and the kitchen.

There is a desk with three vases of roses on it, plus several chairs. A settee and poufs are dotted around the study. On the walls are fencing masks and épées.

Two Jacobean chairs stand by the window. One chair has a gigantic toy Panda on it, and there is a four-foot square object covered with a dust-cloth on the other chair.

Occasionally the sound of the sea can be heard, and the raucous screech of seagulls. A sudden flash of evening sunshine runs across the wine-dark carpet.

The door leading to the garden opens quietly. JOSEPH KING enters. JOSEPH, who is First Secretary to the Minister of Defence, is in his early forties. He is very sure of himself, and proud of his luxuriant, handlebar moustache, which habitually he strokes. He is carrying a briefcase.

JOSEPH: Anyone at home?

> *(From upstairs we hear the grumbling, wheezing voice of GRANDPA.)*

GRANDPA: Me!

JOSEPH: *(Laughing.)* You're not included, Grandpa. Well, you're not really here, are you?

GRANDPA: *(Off.)* That's very true. Unfortunately.

(GRANDPA slams his upstairs door.

Dismissively JOSEPH flings his briefcase onto his desk. Then he whips off his suit jacket, plucks a fencing épée from the wall, hurls his jacket into the air and catches it on the point of his raised épée. Dextrously he slides the jacket off his épée onto his desk chair.

With a flick of his sword, JOSEPH opens the catch of the French windows. He stands a moment gazing at the hissing sea. Then he ducks as a seagull screams over his head. He slashes his sword at the retreating bird.)

JOSEPH: With more practice I could cut that turd-dropping bird in half. *(He moves back into the room and begins his vigorous fencing exercises. He is an excellent swordsman and knows it. Methodically he cuts to pieces the roses in one of the ornate vases on his desk. But as he cuts off the last rose, accidentally he knocks over the vase, which breaks in two.)* Typical. Not enough crudding control. *(In disgust he slams his épée down on the desk. Then he wipes the sweat off his brow, and proceeds to mop the spilt water up with his handkerchief. He is about to throw his now-soaked handkerchief and the broken vase into a wastepaper basket, when the telephone rings loudly on his desk. Guiltily he jumps, dropping his handkerchief and the broken vase onto the floor. He feels the perspiration on his shirt as he hovers over the ringing phone.)* I'm sweating worse than the P.M. But at least that bastard's paid to sweat. *(He picks up the phone.)* Hello, yes… Yes, this is Hythe 1812… Who's speaking?… Oh yes, Miss Tamara Fanghorn… Sorry, but my wife's not back from school yet… No, she's not a pupil, she teaches there!… Yes, you are speaking to Joseph King, and, yes, Jane did mention you were coming to stay, Miss Fanghorn, so I suggest you catch the six o'clock train from Waterloo. Then someone will pick you up from Brighton Station at about seven-fifteen… I don't know; it'll be either Jane, or Jackie, or Joseph – that's me. Or it might be Grandpa, or maybe Wolfy, our Pussy-Dog, or even Humph, the Panda bear. You can never tell in this house…

Yes, I did go to Eton actually, but I fail to see what that's got to do with anything… Of course, I'll tell Jane that you rang. Goodbye, Miss Fanghorn. *(He puts the receiver down.)* Funny woman! But then most funny women are. *(He picks up the broken roses and the pieces of the vase, and he drops them into the wastepaper basket. Then obscuring the shrouded four-foot object on the Jacobean chair with his body, reverently JOSEPH lifts up the dust cloth that is covering the object. He appears to be straightening something that is part of the object, but the Audience can't see what he's doing. Nervously he looks around to see if he's being observed, then he addresses the toy Panda.)* This has nothing to do with you, Humphy! *(There is a knock on the Stage Right door. Guiltily he pulls the dust-sheet down over the object on the chair.)* Yes, what is it?

JACKIE: *(Off.)* It's me, Daddy. Can I come in?

JOSEPH: 'Course, love.

(JACKIE, his daughter, enters. She is an attractive sixteen-year-old in tight-fitting jeans and a figure-hugging top. She gives her father an affectionate kiss on the cheek.)

JACKIE: So how's the First Secretary to the Minister of Defence today?

JOSEPH: Fairly pooped. Though I could feel worse. But tomorrow's the first day of the summer recess, thank God.

JACKIE: By the way, I've just killed Wolfy, Daddy.

JOSEPH: Jolly good.

JACKIE: Yes, Wolfy just hiccuped and dropped dead.

JOSEPH: Did he bleed much?

JACKIE: About as much as a bowl of tomato soup.

JOSEPH: Ah, par for the course, then.

JACKIE: That's just what I thought. There's a Miss Fanghorn coming round some time this evening, isn't there?

JOSEPH: *(Sighing.)* So it seems.

JACKIE: I hope she's not like the rest of Jane's friends. Well, most of 'em are fully-uddered cows. Oh I know I shouldn't be vulgar, Daddy, but I believe in calling a pig in a poke a poked pig. *(In response JOSEPH unhooks another épée from the wall and throws it to her. She catches it deftly.)* Oh not fencing again!

(JOSEPH picks up his épée from the desk.)

JOSEPH: You bet ya. *(Lunging at her.)* So have at you!

JACKIE: *(Parrying clumsily.)* Let me at least get my mask on, or I'll end up dead like poor Wolfy! *(JOSEPH lunges at her again. She leaps to one side, grabs a mask from the wall and runs for cover behind the desk. JOSEPH hesitates because he is worried about smashing the other two rose vases. This gives JACKIE time to put her mask on. As she emerges from behind the desk, he lunges at her.)* No, Dad! My mask's on the wrong way. I can't see a thing!

(With a flick of his fingers, JOSEPH adjusts her mask for her. As he does so, playfully she makes as if she's going to knee him in the groin.)

JOSEPH: You naughty minx. *(He flashes his sword close to her throat.)* Did you cut the Pussy-Dog's throat, and then let the blood drain? But, come to think of it, that's more the Leader of the Opposition's style. Only he was talking about my throat.

JACKIE: *(Giggling.)* No, I just spread arsenic on Wolfy's dog-biscuits.

JOSEPH: But he's a cat. Well, he *was* a cat. Wasn't she?

JACKIE: Yes, and she told me that she liked cat-food, so that's why I gave him dog-biscuits. Well, I'm not going to be a vet for nothing, am I?

(They cross swords. Then immediately he lowers his sword and laughs.)

JACKIE: What's so funny?

JOSEPH: *(Pointing to the window.)* Look at that gull fighting the wind.

(JACKIE looks through the window. JOSEPH touches her breast with the tip of his épée.)

JACKIE: OWW!

JOSEPH: You're growing up in a helluva hurry, aren't you?

JACKIE: That hurt. Well, it did! Mammaries are very sensitive things.

JOSEPH: I bet your Greek teacher never told you that Amazon women cut their very left sensitive things off so they could draw their bows back to the full. And savour all those other Saphic delights.

JACKIE: *(Beginning to fence with him.)* D'you think Jane would approve of you being so suggestive?

JOSEPH: No. So?

JACKIE: So don't, Daddy. D'you like my jeans? Incredibly tight, aren't they?

JOSEPH: Yes, and you think they make you look like a boy, don't you? But that's the very last thing they do.

JACKIE: Oh come on, they make me look butch, extraordinarily tough and as sexy as all get out.

(JACKIE fences energetically to prove her point, but it is obvious that JOSEPH could beat her whenever he wants to.)

JOSEPH: Did you see Mummy at school today?

JACKIE: Step-Mummy!

JOSEPH: Alright, if you have to be judicious about it – Step-Mummy. *(He lowers his épée.)* But I do wish you'd try to think about Janey as your Mum.

JACKIE: I do. 'Cause she's much better than my real mother. In fact , if you remember, I celebrated your divorce from Mother with seven very large bottles of Coke.

JOSEPH: Yes, and then you were promptly sick all night.

JACKIE: And also Janey's pretty dishy, whereas Mother Mary was about as sexy as London Transport.

JOSEPH: I happen to like London Transport. And not just because my Party supports it.

JACKIE: Obviously. Otherwise you wouldn't have married a double-decker.

JOSEPH: Jackie!

JACKIE: Anyway Janey cares for me. Well, she does! As much as any woman is capable of caring for something she didn't give birth to.

JOSEPH: You should go to the flicks tonight. I've heard, with a little queuing, you might even get into 'Dracula With The Hots'.

JACKIE: Daddy, why do you always change the subject when I try to be profound?

JOSEPH: Because instinct and love are a woman's best weapons, dear.

JACKIE: *(Flaunting her breasts.)* A minute ago you were trying to cut my best weapons off.

JOSEPH: I think it's time for jumpies to counteract cheekies.

JACKIE: Oh no!

JOSEPH: Yes; up! Up!

(He swings his épée in a cutting arc towards her legs. As his blade flashes beneath her, she jumps just in time over his épée.)

JACKIE: I don't want to do jumpies!

JOSEPH: Then you shouldn't be so lippy.

(He makes her jump again.)

JACKIE: No, Daddy!

(She jumps.)

JOSEPH: There's no training like it. This is part... *(She jumps.)* ...of the Junior Sex... *(She jumps.)* ...Limbering-Up Course... *(She jumps.)* ...made justly famous by certain Lords... *(She jumps.)* ...in the House of Lords.

JACKIE: But they can't do a Junior Sex... *(She jumps.)* ...Limbering-Up Course in the House of Lords. I thought most of 'em were doddering old codgers.

JOSEPH: Indeed, they are, my poppet, but that doesn't stop 'em periodically trying to limber up their withered loins. No resting now!

JACKIE: *(Jumping over his swishing épée.)* Oh, no, no, no!

JOSEPH: And surely I told you how I discovered the Minister of Health wheezing under the Minister of Labour?

(She jumps.)

JACKIE: No, you didn't; so don't! It all sounds terribly messy. *(Now completely exhausted she collapses on a pouf, hugging the huge Panda bear.)* Oh Humph, I haven't even been bedded, and yet I'm totally deaded!

(There is a scratching noise on the Stage Left door. JOSEPH opens it. JANE, his 25 year-old wife, staggers into the room, laden down with shopping which inadvertently she spills all over the floor. JANE is wearing baby-blue jeans like her step-daughter, but her clothes are doused in acrylic and oil paint.)

JOSEPH: Hello, darling. Your Fanghorn friend said she'd be at the station in two-and-a-half hours' time.

JANE: *(Indicating the groceries strewn all over the carpet.)* For God's sake, Joseph, now that Parliament's in recess, can't you at least be useful at home for once, and give me a hand with all this?

JOSEPH: *(Helping her.)* Of course, darling. But I did say *you'd* pick up Fanghorn – as she's your friend.

JANE: Joseph, you're the bloody limit!

JOSEPH: Well, she must be someone's friend. *(He throws JACKIE her discarded foil. JACKIE drops it.)* Butter fingers. We must keep on our toes if we're going to stay fit for what's coming.

JANE: *(Still on her knees picking up the spilt shopping.)* Please, no more duelling, Joseph. I've got one helluva headache coming on. Ow! Now I've cut my bloody self! But that's impossible. There's no glass here. Well, there shouldn't be. Oh no! It's from my favourite vase.

JOSEPH: *(With a nervous laugh.)* Funny you should say that, darling, but just before you came in, the wind suddenly sprang up to Force 7 – or even 8. I hadn't got a gauge at the time, but the weathercock went mad. And the next thing I knew, the vase was blown – tinkle! tinkle! – onto the carpet. Then perversely one second later, it dropped down to Force 1. *(He thrusts an outstretched wet finger into the air.)* And now the guilty old wind has slunk back to sea.

JANE: Really, you and your preposterous stories are endlessly tiresome. Especially as I've had such a terrible day trying to teach little bitches and little bastards, not to mention little in-betweens, the glories of Renoir Pere. And unfortunately that only put one idea into their dirty little minds, and I wasn't having any of that going on in my classroom. Anyway, why does everything have to reduce itself to sex? Give me a class of just girls any day. I can't be doing with having to teach this assortment of dolly-mixtures.

(JACKIE helps JANE to pile the shopping back into the bags. Then JACKIE sits JANE down on a pouf, and she folds the giant Panda bear in JANE's arms.)

JACKIE: Poor little Janey.

JOSEPH: *(Who is now trying to break his sword in contrition.)* I'll break my sword, my darling, to show my abject contrition for windily lying to you about the fate of your favourite vase.

JANE: Oh don't be such a thespian klutz. You're supposed to be the First Secretary to something or other, aren't you? – so, for once, act your age!

JOSEPH: What a thing to ask of an Englishman.

JANE: Well, you're certainly going to need to, with what's coming.

JOSEPH: What are you on about now, darling? *(JACKIE jabs his backside with her épée.)* OWWW!

JACKIE: That'll teach you, meanie.

JANE: Oh for God's sake, both of you, stop it! I really can't take anymore of your asinine games.

(JANE sits on the sofa and purposefully folds her arms. JOSEPH crosses to her, unfolds her arms and sits on JANE's knee.)

JOSEPH: Give us a kiss, my lovely. The French variety, with a preponderance of tongue. Then I promise I'll be a good boy. Oh come on, baby. You know you love a saliva-joust just as much as I do; so let's get tongue-sandwiching.

(He kisses JANE passionately while JACKIE looks on with a certain amount of distaste. JANE comes up for air. JOSEPH tries to kiss her again, but JANE opens her legs, enforcing JOSEPH to fall between her legs onto the floor.)

JANE: Now that's more than enough. Inordinate sexual gratification is all you seem to be interested in.

JOSEPH: Have I ever denied it? More and more sex is what I say; onto the Advanced Course!

JACKIE: I'm probably a bit backwards in regard to the Karma Sutra, Daddy, but I'm told that I'm a real hit in the missionary position.

JOSEPH: My God!

JACKIE: There's no need to bring irrelevance into it.

JANE: Look, Joseph, why don't you give this childish, knockabout humour of yours a permanent rest? It's a total waste of life. 'Cause Jackie and I know what's *really* bothering you. So shall we all chant it together? One!

JACKIE: Two!

JANE/JACKIE: Three!

JANE/JACKIE/JOSEPH: CHINA!!!

JOSEPH: Well, it is a problem. A Chinese problem.

JACKIE: *(Groaning.)* Here we go again.

JOSEPH: No, no, I'm being very serious, because you don't know what I learned today…

JACKIE: *(Overriding him.)* And we don't want to!

JOSEPH: It'll be in all the papers in the morning. The Chinese People's Republic has so many mouths to feed and nowhere to expand, so Mao Tse Tung's been indoctrinating the Chinese to believe that they should explode over their borders.

JACKIE: But what's all that got to with us, Daddy? It's China!

JOSEPH: Yes, but the Chinese need Lebensraum far more badly than old Adolf and Tojo ever did, and so Mao means to have it. Yes, and we received a communiqué from his Foreign Secretary informing us of the inevitability of India becoming part of China. And, furthermore, he warned us that if we took any steps to prevent an invasion of India, then indiscriminate bombing would take place within twenty-four hours in Europe and America. Of course we question whether the Chinese have any weapons capable of achieving the necessary distance and accuracy to penetrate our Defence installations. But the rest of Europe's another matter. Devastation is perpetually on its doorstep. Bombs, rats and blood always remain as an imminent prospect to destroy all the gleaming glass and steel of recently-resurrected Berlin.

JANE: Does it help you to chat away to yourself like this, dear?

JOSEPH: My lambs, it's because of Soviet and Chinese Communism that two thirds of the world are now clamped in the thumbscrews of dictatorship where the ruthless supremacy of the mind relentlessly squashes the messiness of the human heart. Yes, and they're after *your* heart, Jane, and mine, and yours, Jackie. See, Communists, unlike ourselves, aren't hooked by religion – other than the religion of world domination. So crucifixions and resurrections are only fatuous reactionary symbols to the millions of Russians and Chinese who want to chop up millions of Russians and Chinese in Russia and China.

JANE: Yes, but what the hell are *you* going to do about it all?

JOSEPH: Britain can only do little things now; like shout, threaten, wait, and provide some shelters, hospitals and rehabilitation. That's, of course, if there's anyone left to rehabilitate. Our tragedy is that we have built an atomic-world-ender; so we're much worse than Nature. She only gives us an injection of volcanic fire, wind and water when she senses the need for some balance in her world. Whereas we do it when we get bored with ordinary death. As if we didn't have enough on our plates with cancer, heart attacks, leprosy, typhoid and homelessness. Yes, this is a lecture! Because I've got to say something to the Minister when he phones me – as he surely will. Especially if China decides to rape and pillage India! So I've got to find different words for the same old problems. Though that fat bastard'll want more than words. But I haven't got anything else but a lot of shabby words to cover up our national impotence.

(Pause. Then JANE and JACKIE proceed to give a derisory, slow hand-clap.)

JANE: You just made all that Chinese tosh up on the spur of the moment, didn't you?

JOSEPH: Yes, and under the circumstances, I thought I did it rather well. So now let's have some dinner.

JACKIE: Daddy, was that just another of your innumerable shaggy-dog stories without a tail?

JOSEPH: *(Laughing.)* Recently we have had vague rumblings from China, of course, but, yes, you're right. The rest of it was only a joke. Mind, it has made me feel incredibly peckish. So, girls, why don't you both sashay your way into the kitchen and concoct us a little delectable something or other? Like Lobster Napoleon or Thai Dublin Bay Prawns. Nothing too ambitious.

JANE: Typical. The Lord commands and his handmaidens rustle their breasts between their knees in obsequious abeyance.

JOSEPH: Mmmm…familial erotica. There's nothing quite like it. Or would you prefer to have a fencing knockabout before dinner?

JANE: Absolutely not! I've had fifteen months of you and this marriage and your fencing and knockabouts and you!

JOSEPH: What kind of sentence is that?

JANE: Let's duff up the little rotter, Jackie.

(JANE and JACKIE grab their épées, and simultaneously launch themselves at JOSEPH, who defends himself with his foil.)

JOSEPH: Mutiny! Treason!

JACKIE/JANE: Sexual equality!

JOSEPH: That'll be the day. *(Defending himself he backs his way towards the window.)* Oh this is just like old times, Janey, when I met you at the Fencing Club. But unfortunately you've developed a bit of a pot since then, my darling.

JANE: You priapic prick!

JACKIE: Yes, let's dart the pompous ponce against the wall, Janey!

(As they attack, JANE accidentally knocks another bowl of roses onto the carpet.)

JOSEPH: Two down, Missy. One more to go, and you win the Prize of a dead mouse in a goldfish bowl. Or if you prefer – an over-stuffed Panda Bear!

(From upstairs we hear GRANDPA's voice.)

GRANDPA: *(Off.)* Who's killing my daughter?

JANE: Don't worry, I'm still alive, Dad. *(JOSEPH lunges at JANE, and misses her.)* But only just.

GRANDPA: *(Off.)* More to the point. Where's my dinner? I'm ravenous.

JACKIE: Oh Grandpa, can't you give your stomach a rest for once?

JANE: No, he can't help it. That's why vegetarians live longer than everyone else because they always seem to be hungrier than the rest of us.

(The Stage Right door, leading to the stairs, bursts open and the fuming figure of GRANDPA enters. He is a foul-mouthed, engaging, energetic old man, with baggy trousers that are held up by bright-red braces. As he comes into the room, simultaneously JOSEPH disarms JANE and JACKIE.)

JOSEPH: If only diplomacy was as simple as disarming you two, then we'd still be a great nation instead of merely being an American satellite.

JANE: Or a Chinese satellite.

GRANDPA: Now you three make up and be friends. All this rapacious fighting! Your mother and me never had a cross word, our Janey. Well, not often. Not very often. I didn't murder her immediately she crossed me. Just the moment after. Which was nearly all the time. Well, you expect to be murdered if you make me salads with cabbage instead of lettuce. Trouble was, your mother could never tell the difference. 'Well, they're both green,' she said. 'So's my grass,' I said. Then she told me not to swear. As if I've ever made a mistake in swearing. I know 'arse' is me sewerage quarters and 'grass' is what I wipe it with, and I don't care for either of 'em in me salad.

JACKIE: You're rambling again, Grandpa.

GRANDPA: Balls. I'm just exerting the warmth of me personality. More to the point; I've shelled all the peas for tonight's dinner which should be on the table pronto 'cause I'm still bloody starving.

JANE: I didn't see the peas on the table, Dad.

GRANDPA: 'Course you didn't. You'd be very clever to see 'em where they weren't, wouldn't you?

JANE: *(Taking a pack of cigarettes out of her handbag.)* Oh no more games, please, Dad. Where are the pigging peas?

GRANDPA: *(Rubbing his stomach.)* In here.

JANE: *(Lighting her cigarette.)* You haven't eaten all of them!

GRANDPA: I have.

JANE: Greedy-guts!

(She takes a hasty puff.)

JOSEPH: Don't smoke, dear. *(He takes the cigarette from her and stubs it out in the bowl of roses.)* It's bad for the roses.

JANE: But the peas were a major part of our dinner, Dad.

GRANDPA: They're not now. So I hope you've bought some more 'cause I'm still ruddy starving.

JANE: Oh Mummy, where are you?

(JANE exits into the kitchen.)

GRANDPA: Yes, it's all on its way, Joseph. I feel the spring tightening. 'Cause you've got to pay for exuding years and years of vitriol and bad breath in Parliament. And I certainly don't like the dead voices trapped in your socks and your tie. So would you kindly ask 'em to leave?

JOSEPH: *(Putting his épée back on the wall.)* You're not real, are you, Grandpus? You're just an over-wound-up talk-box.

GRANDPA: *(To JANE.)* But I do miss yer Mum, our Janey. Poor old cow. Though still I wish she wouldn't haunt me. Every night she comes out of her grave and gives me GBH of the lughole. Makes sleeping so tricky. But she has warned me what's coming. *(He takes the largest apple from the fruit bowl and stuffs it into his mouth.)* God, I'm always so horrendously hungry. So she used to feed me on seaweed.

JACKIE: Why ever did she do that, Grandpa?

GRANDPA: She read somewhere that it was poisonous. So where is this Fanghorn that's coming to purr, or sleep, or whatever you do when the moon's cold? 'Cause this is the waiting time, see. But are *you* ready for it, Joseph? *(He throws his half-eaten apple which hits JOSEPH on the side of the head.)* Obviously not.

JOSEPH: Now cut that out, you old bastard. This is my house, and I...

GRANDPA: *(Overriding him.)* I know. You bought it and you own it. Like you own me daughter, and me step-granddaughter. So are you're going to throw me out on the streets again, Joe? 'Cause we usually come round to that after six days of truce, or truth, or whatever you like to call it.

JOSEPH: Look, I didn't mean to threaten you, Grandpa. I've just had such a pig of a day arguing the pros and cons of China.

GRANDPA: Well, that's real dumb of you, Joe, 'cause China's the up and coming, sonny, while you're the down and going.

JACKIE: I killed Wolfy this afternoon, Grandpa.

GRANDPA: No, no, you couldn't have, Jackie! Where'd you leave him? Not on the beach, with the wind twingeing him.

JACKIE: I cut his throat with a pea-opener. Yes, with that new gadget that Jane bought to shell those peas that you've just noshed. *(Demonstrating.)* Ricky-icky-rip! Just like that. And Wolfy went woof-purr-woof, gurgle-gurgle, and dropped down dead at my feet.

JOSEPH: *(Reading a newspaper.)* So put that in your salad and smoke it.

GRANDPA: I can't bear cats in me salad. Worse than boiled cabbage.

JOSEPH: You'll go insane if you go on like that, Grandpus. So why don't you shufty off and find Wolfy? Then give him a decent burial. There's a nice little spot in the lettuce patch where we buried…you know what.

GRANDPA: I can't bear cruelty to vegetables. And, anyroad, you'll make me as nutty as you are, if you go on like this.

JOSEPH: But you'll never tell anyone our little secret about the lettuce patch, will you, Grandpa? Or I will really throw you out.

GRANDPA: No, never. It's such a lovely, horrid secret.

JACKIE: What secret's that, Dad?

JOSEPH: I'll share it with you when you're older.

GRANDPA: Tell me where you've put our Wolfy. Please, Jackie!

JOSEPH: He's sponging somewhere in Cat Hell – like his recent owner.

GRANDPA: Look, I didn't mean all that about what's coming, Joseph, so don't be mean to me. Well, I suppose there's nothing for it. I'd better go and find Wolfy meself.

(GRANDPA exits into the garden.)

JOSEPH: Daddy, why are you always so cruel to Grandpa? Is it because he's not ours and just a porcine snuffler?

JOSEPH: Did you truly kill Wolfy?

JACKIE: 'Course I didn't. I'm quite fond of Wolfy really. Can I show you something, Daddy?

JOSEPH: Is it rude or crude or anything?

JACKIE: No, it's just…something. Now watch carefully. *(She gets down on her hands and knees.)* I wouldn't do this for anyone else. *(She springs into a handstand. Then very slowly she jerkily begins to walk on her hands towards him.)* You should join me, Daddy. Interesting view.

JOSEPH: Yes, I suppose there is a different perspective that way up. A kingdom of carpet piling, smelly feet and upside-down groins.

(She lowers herself to the ground.)

JACKIE: You're not supposed to laugh, meanie.

JOSEPH: Yes, but what's the point? I mean, what is it meant to mean?

JACKIE: Nothing. It *is.* That is the point. It's just part of the evening.

(JACKIE springs into another handstand. Simultaneously the door leading to the garden opens and TAMARA FANGHORN enters. She is tall, dark and very handsome, with gleaming teeth. She is wearing the traditional, figure-hugging, long black leather dress.)

TAMARA: The old man's just been sick. *(Savouring JACKIE and her handstand.)* How enchantingly provocative. *(JACKIE collapses in a heap. TAMARA shakes JACKIE by the foot.)* How do you do? I'm extremely well, thank you.

JOSEPH: *(Disconcerted.)* But you can't arrive yet, Miss er… I mean…I beg your pardon.

TAMARA: I hope that's the only thing you'll be begging, Joseph.

JOSEPH: But you're not supposed to be arriving for at least a couple of hours…

TAMARA: Shall I go back then? *(To JACKIE.)* Beautiful child. You're Jackie, aren't you? *(Shaking JOSEPH's hand.)* You look very well yourself, Joseph. I'm Tamara Fanghorn, Heir to the Winter of Drachfells, but my friends call me Tammers and sometimes Fangers. *(She produces a copy of the Evening Standard from her bag.)* Thought you'd like to see the evening newspaper, Joseph. *(She shows the headlines to JOSEPH.)* Isn't it lovely? Apparently China's preparing for imminent war with India.

JOSEPH: *(Snatching the paper from her.)* Impossible!

TAMARA: I knew you'd like it. It's all on its way now. May I sit down? *(Sitting in his desk chair.)* Thank you. Nice apples. *(She picks up an apple from the fruit bowl and crunches into it.)* No, bit tough. Not so nice. *(After another bite.)* But it will do for the time as most things have to. *(Slipping off her shoes.)* Hope you don't mind but my toes get terribly squashed when they're all together in the same room.

JOSEPH: *(Shaking the paper.)* They're just guessing about China, 'cause I made it all up about there being a possible invasion. It was a kind of sick joke.

TAMARA: *The Evening Standard* rarely has a sense of humour on the front page. 'Fact *The Standard* rarely has a sense of humour. Joseph – I may call you 'Joseph', mayn't I? I mean, you were christened 'Joseph', weren't you? It's not another lie, is it? An Arctic lie looking for the Sahara. Talking of Arctic… *(To JACKIE.)* I'd like a vodka and lime with three iceberg cubes, if you please.

JACKIE: *(Hypnotised by TAMARA, she shakes hands with her.)* How – with three iceberg cubes – do you do? Yes…

(Perplexed JACKIE exits into the kitchen.)

JOSEPH: *(Throwing the paper down.)* This is just some stupid leak.

TAMARA: Mmmm…the potential's enormous… *(Pointing to the window.)* All that sea and the whaling season to come. Not to mention the barracuda, a fisher of men, and how's your father?

JOSEPH: Dead.

TAMARA: I know, but how?

JOSEPH: Where the hell's Jane? And how'd you get here so quickly?

TAMARA: I was already here when I rang you.

JOSEPH: *(Astonished.)* You were already here when you…?

TAMARA: Yes, I rang you from the old man's room.

JOSEPH: *(Pointing.)* You rang me from up there?

TAMARA: Nice old codger. *(Licking her lips provocatively.)* But he doesn't understand the ecstasy of swallowing blood. He only eats vegetable decay. But we still had a very instructive conversation. Pity his breath reeked of rotting cabbage.

JOSEPH: Look, I don't regard any of this as funny.

TAMARA: Jane said you'd laugh your head off. Literally. Especially about China and Comrade Mao. *(Abruptly she turns her head away, covering her nose with both hands.)* Quick! Give me your handkerchief. I suffer from the most chronic nose-bleeds.

JOSEPH: *(Smiling and not moving.)* Funny. I haven't got one.

(TAMARA grabs some tissues from the desk and applies them to her nose.)

TAMARA: It's the excess of blood trying to get out. And it always happens over the port.

JOSEPH: *(Relenting and going to her.)* Look, I'm sorry, Tamara. I didn't mean to be callous. *(Shouting into the kitchen.)* Jane, for God's sake, get in here! *(To TAMARA.)* I'm just not very good at things like this. *(bellowing.)* Jane!!!

(He helps TAMARA to her feet.)

TAMARA: *(Sarcastically.)* Oh, a genuine gentleman.

JOSEPH: JANE!!!

(JANE enters, holding a bowl of potato peelings.)

JANE: Are you alright, darling?

JOSEPH: Well, actually no!

JANE: I didn't mean you. *(Putting the bowl down.)* I meant Darling Tamara. *(She puts her arm around TAMARA's shoulders.)* Come along, sweetheart. I'll show you where the bathroom is.

TAMARA: *(Pressing the tissues against her nose and grinning.)* But I know where it is, Janey Baby, don't I? *(Exiting towards the stairs.)* But then you can be such a gorgeous dumb-dumb.

JANE: *(Shouting after her.)* When you've cleaned yourself up, love, go and have a little lie-down, and I'll bring you some soup, and Jackie'll come up with your vodka.

TAMARA: *(Off.)* Don't forget the lime and the three iceberg cubes.

JOSEPH: *(Furious.)* Jane, I think I deserve an explanation!

JANE: Explanation?

JOSEPH: Yes, an explanation!

JANE: *(Sniffing.)* Oh dear, the brussels are boiling over.
(Shouting off.) Jackie, turn the stove down.

JOSEPH: I demand a fornicating explanation!

JANE: Do you want roast potatoes, boiled potatoes, sauté
potatoes, French fries or pommes de terre.

JOSEPH: Why didn't you tell me that this woman who has a
penchant for nose-bleeds has already been in my house for
the last couple of hours?

JANE: Days.

JOSEPH: Days?!!

JANE: And actually we haven't got any potatoes, so…

JOSEPH: What d'you mean 'days'? Look, why, in God's name
didn't you tell me…?

JANE: *(Overriding him.)* Because Dad's just eaten them. *(She
picks up the bowl of potato-peelings and waves them under his
nose.)* All he has left you are the potato-peelings and the
eyes – which look like your sweet little blackheads.

JOSEPH: What the bloody hell's going on around here?

JANE: Garlic salad. It should go very nicely with the chop suey.

JOSEPH: It sounds dreadful. Look, when you say 'days'? What
d'you mean by 'days'?

JANE: *(Going towards the kitchen.)* Tamara's been here for
the last two days, so she could see where to begin.
Experiments on humans are very tricky things, dear.

(JANE disappears down the passageway.)

JOSEPH: *(Shouting after her.)* Experiments on humans? What
humans? Answer me, Jane. Janey! Woman! Bloody
woman! *(Frenziedly he gives the wastepaper basket a kick.)* I
don't know why you put up with it, Joseph King. After

all, you are a V.I.P. You're a copper-bottomed VIP! *(He snatches the newspaper from his desk.)* And on top of it all, there's the Yellow Bleeding Peril! Because, for once, perhaps *The Standard's* got something right *(He picks up the telephone and shouts down it.)* Miss Cherub! *(Then he realises he has forgotten to dial, so he dials.)* God, I'm in such a state, I forgot to dial. I've completely lost the plot. *(Into the phone.)* Miss Cherub, that you?.... Yes, and I need to speak to the Minister at once, Miss Cherub. *(Shouting into the phone.)* Look, I don't care whether you're about to be taken short, Miss Cherub, but I've got to...

(JANE puts her head around the door.)

JANE: Why do you always have to shout your politics, dear? It only gives the distinct impression that you're insecure. *(She disappears again, but she leaves the door open as she calls down the corridor.)* Oh there you are, Tamara darling.

JOSEPH: *(Into the receiver.)* Look, Miss Cherub, the Minister told me he was going to have lunch with the Chinese Ambassador, Mr Huang Chang Ho, so it shouldn't be too difficult to find him now... What?...

TAMARA: *(Off.)* I feel so much better, Janey Baby, and the chop suey, garlic salad, and vodka and lime with three iceberg cubes will settle my stomach a treat.

JOSEPH: *(Shouting towards the kitchen.)* Yes, and a human experiment with chop suey to you, too! *(Hastily into the phone.)* No, no, I certainly don't mean you, Miss Cherub. I'm just under a lot of stress because of my recently-acquired splitting headache. *(Now shouting into the phone.)* No, I don't think a couple of Aspirins is the answer, and I'm not bloody shouting, Miss Angel Cherub, Goddamit! *(He slams the phone down.)* And don't grin at me, you two-timing pandering Mandarin!

(He gives the Panda bear a hearty kick as JACKIE comes in from the kitchen, swigging back a large glass of red wine.)

JACKIE: Dinner's ready, Daddy. It's burnt, it's cold and there isn't much of it 'cause Grandpa's eaten all the beansprouts but Janey says it's dinner and she's my Step-Mummy, so who am I to argue?

(JACKIE exits.)

JOSEPH: Jesus wept. *(To the Panda bear.)* And even *you* can see why He would!

(Having checked that he's alone, JOSEPH picks up a discarded épée. He uses its point to carefully lift up the dust-cover that is covering the object on the chair. But the Audience still can't see what it is.

JANE enters, carrying a tray with JOSEPH's meal on it. Hastily JOSEPH pulls the dust-cover down over the object. Then he moves back into the centre of the room, swishing his épée.

JANE plonks the tray at his feet, and takes a knife and fork from his desk and clatters them onto the tray.)

JANE: Joseph, I've had all your complaints up to here, and I've swigged down two large vodkas and lime, and now I don't care a bugger, so you can stuff it!

(Triumphantly she slams out of the room, and goes back into the kitchen.)

JOSEPH: Janey! What the devil's up with you now? *(He examines his meal with the tip of his épée.)* Chop suey and garlic salad all on the same plate. Ugh, it looks so puke-worthy, it's trying to crawl off. And there's no way I can get away from it!

(He looks up to see…TAMARA, who has just entered. She is dabbing her nose with a blood-stained handkerchief in one hand, while she holds a large jug in the other.)

TAMARA: Talking to yourself again. Noteworthy.

JOSEPH: As I said, I just can't get away from it!

TAMARA: Accept it. The Greeks did.

JOSEPH: But I'm not a Greek, and I'm not Chinese! I'm…

TAMARA: *(Finishing his sentence.)* …under a plot-losing strain. My nose isn't still spurting, is it? *(Waving the jug at him.)* But don't worry, I've done my best to keep most of my blood out of the salad dressing I've just made you. So you'll absolutely adore it. Especially as I've added some rare herbs to it that have a nose-twitching fragrance. Sniff!

JOSEPH: Do I really have to?

TAMARA: *(Thrusting the jug under his nose.)* I said 'sniff'!

JOSEPH: *(Pulling away after sniffing.)* Incredible. It smells just like incense. But I don't want to go the church when I have my dinner. *(She pours the salad-dressing liberally over his chop suey.)* And I certainly don't want incense all over my chop suey! Anyway, what the hell did you put in it?

TAMARA: The entrails of ecstasy and chopped diamonds.

JOSEPH: What you do for a living?

TAMARA: Pelicans' tonsils.

JOSEPH: I mean, during the day.

TAMARA: But the prime ingredient is rhino's horn – *(Handing him the tray.)* – mixed up, of course, with arsenic.

(He plonks the tray on his desk.)

JOSEPH: What are you? I mean, specifically? In the long run? What's twisting you like this? The sea air? *(Above the sound of a seagull.)* That gannet's screech? Wormwood? Goddamit, now I'm beginning to chunter like you! And what's even more disconcerting, you remind me of someone…of…

TAMARA: Your father?

JOSEPH: That's the second time you've mentioned him. Why the interest? And there is something sitting in your eyes! *(Hysteria begins to set in.)* So I'd be obliged if you'd leave this house immediately. And that thing that's sitting in your eyes, would you kindly tell it to stand up when I'm talking?!

(TAMARA laughs as she pours herself a glass of port.)

TAMARA: Look, I'm only trying to help you into the new ways, Joseph. I mean… after your childhood tripods and the nitric acid stains around your Bunsen burner, and all those years of continuous chemical change, when no one's there – inside your brain, Joseph. Those wasted moments of void – between the end of your last thought and the beginning of the next – yes, in those midnight moments; when the most horrific things can get inside your head and play havoc with your imagination. *(Savouring her glass of port.)* Mmm…this vintage port is nearly as delectable as blood. Because, you see, Joe, it's when you think that you're *not* thinking that all the evil in the world can get inside your skull. And then the malefic things begin to grow there…

(In desperation JOSEPH hugs the Panda bear.)

JOSEPH: She's not really here, is she, Humph? She must be something I've made up. A wet dream with nose-bleeds, incense and something sitting in your eyes! Will you kindly tell it to stand up!?

(Now giggling violently TAMARA pours herself some more port.)

TAMARA: Oh it's going to be more delectable than downing several pints of blood, with an aphrodisiac as a chaser. You've just no idea of the delectable pain that's coming your way. Now eat your arsenic before it gets cold. *(The telephone rings.)* What's that?

JOSEPH: Some idiot imitating the telephone!

TAMARA: *(Pointing to the covered object on the chair.)* No, that.

JOSEPH: *(Picking up the receiver.)* Hello? *(Gesturing frenziedly at TAMARA.)* Please don't touch it, Tamara! Don't, please… *(Into the phone.)* Hello?…

TAMARA: *(Peeping under the dust-cover and giggling.)* Yes, I always sensed the basic fear seething under your political enamel. But the truth is, Joe, you've totally lost it.

JOSEPH: *(Into the phone.)* Yes, it is me, Minister, but…

(TAMARA exits towards the kitchen, calling over her shoulder.)

TAMARA: You pre-pubescent, little Jesus man you!

JOSEPH: *(Into the phone.)* Look, Minister, I'm very sorry you had to over-hear all that female, jackass hysteria but, you see… No, it wasn't the cat. She's dead. I mean, he's dead. The cat, that is. 'Least I think she, he or it is! But in this house you can never tell!…. Yes, I know it's all irrelevant but how did this catastrophic mess happen?… What?.. But it's impossible for the Chinese Ambassador to become inebriated at lunch? We always water the Scotch down, don't we?… Huang Chang Ho brought his own Saki. The cheek of these Orientals… Then Ho lurched out of your Club and was promptly sick over *The Evening Standard* reporter's sandals. Oh my God… Now let me get this right. Then Huang Chang Ho said to the reporter; 'If you promise not to publish the vomiting edition, then I will give you some real news.' And then Ho added as a kind of perverse joke; 'China's going to declare war on India in the morning.' *(JOSEPH laughs hysterically.)* No, I don't think it's funny, Minister, I'm just having hysterics… Yes, yes, of course, I'll come back as quick as poss. But, in the interim, surely you can persuade Haung Chang Ho to retract everything he's said about China going to war with India?… What?! Ho has just dropped down dead of alcoholic poisoning…. Yes, yes, of course, Minister, I'm coming immediately. If not before! *(He puts the phone down, and frantically stuffs some chop suey and garlic salad into his mouth as he addresses the Panda bear.)* Fanghorn wouldn't really try to poison me, would she, Humphy?

(Still eating, JOSEPH fights his way into his suit jacket as GRANDPA enters via the door to the kitchen.)

GRANDMA: I can't stand it! Fangers is here to stay! She just said so, and I was the only one to object. Well, it's been bad enough having to sleep with her two nights on the trot. I mean, in the same bed. I'm too old for the strain. And, anyroad, why has Fangers put all that stuff in my bedroom?

JOSEPH: *(Moving to the door as he continues to check through his briefcase.)* What stuff? Oh what the hell's it matter? Hm! Funny...but my stomach does feel a touch...wonky.

GRANDPA: Hardly surprising. Two of the bottles she stashed in my room are definitely arsenic.

JOSEPH: *(Gulping.)* Really?

(JOSEPH exits. GRANDPA tips the rest of JOSEPH's meal down his throat.

Then we hear JACKIE and JANE singing tipsily; 'The Marseillaise'. They break off singing to shout 'Goodnight and good riddance' to JOSEPH as he leaves the house.

Then the tipsy JACKIE and JANE enter singing; 'For he's a jolly bad fellow, and so say all of us, and so say all of us.' TAMARA brings up the rear, and she is completely sober.)

TAMARA: *(To GRANDPA.)* Off with you, Grandpussy! We girls have got to get the flames going.

(They laugh in unison.)

GRANDPA: Alright, alright, I'm high-tailing outta here. But I'll show you. One day very soon, I'll drop dead on you!

TAMARA: That could be very convenient. *(We hear the raucous screaming of dozens of seagulls.)* Oh yes....it's coming!!!

(Black out.)

SCENE TWO

It is now one in the morning in JOSEPH's study.

The windows have been covered with black drapes that are decorated with small red crucifixes.

Moussorgsky's 'Night on a Bare Mountain' is blaring out from JACKIE's battered gramophone, which is on JOSEPH's desk.

JACKIE is now very drunk, and frenziedly she is trying to jive to 'Night on a Bare Mountain'.

TAMARA, who is still sober, is lying on her stomach, and erotically savouring JACKIE's dancing. TAMARA has a large collection of albums beside her.

A moment later GRANDPA and JANE enter through the door leading to the stairs. They are panting as they laboriously lug a large table, covered with a crimson cloth, into the study.

GRANDPA: Ridiculous keeping this in my bedroom. Well, it was very uncomfortable and highly precarious sleeping under this thing. *(He points at TAMARA.)* With her! She's a big woman, y'know. Everywhere I tossed and turned, I ran into another bit of her. Some of the bits were acceptable but most of 'em were positively indecent. What d'you want this bleeding table for, anyway? And where d'you want it?

TAMARA: *(Pointing to a vacant area.)* There will do just fine.

GRANDPA: *(As he and JANE drag the table over to where TAMARA has indicated.)* And now I want to know where Wolfy's body is. And I'm sure Wolfy wants to know, too. So be good girls and tell us.

JANE: Can't you ever give your rambling a rest, Dad?

GRANDPA: Look, our Janey, if you don't tell me where Wolfy is, I'll…well, I'll set your dead mother on you! That'll worry you. Scares me rigid. The Dead are a bit pongy at the best of times. And with all those worms wriggling out of her, Mary Mother of Jesus!

JANE: *(Exiting to the stairs.)* We need another bottle.

GRANDPA: *(Shouting after her.)* What have you done with poor old Wolfy?

TAMARA: Go to bed, Grandpussy. You're travelling again.

GRANDPA: I suppose you want me to go to bed so you can get this experiment of yours going. But I don't approve. And, anyroad, how am I going to sleep with the light bulb in me eyes? You know I can't sleep with the light off, our Janey, 'cause I get the vampire heeby-jeebs. And this table over my head kept the light off me in bed. Even though it was precarious.

JACKIE: Go back to bed, Grandpa.

GRANDPA: I suppose you want me to go back to bed. Well, then to spite you – I'm going.

(GRANDPA exits towards the stairs. During GRANDPA's rambling, TAMARA has unsuccessfully been trying to stroke JACKIE's gyrating ankles as JACKIE drunkenly dances in front of her.)

JACKIE: *(Badly slurring her words.)* Oh…I'm so tiddled and piddled and pished… Hope I'm not going to be ill…

TAMARA: When are you going to come down to London, Jackie? When are you going to try it?

JACKIE: What? Shobering up, you mean?

TAMARA: You can stay with me in my place. Then we can play some real games together. Leapfrog and blind-woman's-bluff and kiss me quick. And that's just the foreplay.

(JACKIE tries to keep her balance as TAMARA attempts to pull her down onto the rug.)

JACKIE: Can we play handshtands? *(TAMARA manages to pull JACKIE down beside her. Then she turns JACKIE's face towards her.)* Mmm, Tamara…you do schmell quite nice… yes, most nice…of port and roshes…

TAMARA: Then gaze into the deep seas of my eyes… *(Imitating JACKIE's slurred speech.)* …where the nichest things will smother you in roshe petals. *(Hypnotically.)* But first you have to journey through the spiral smoke of my irises… into the libidinous darkness of my mind…and the pain you're experiencing is so vivid, but only for a moment – because now you are gazing at the lascivious, naked paintings on the inner walls of my skull; so…open yourself to me, Jacqueline, and be…filled…to satiety…

(TAMARA tries to kiss JACKIE, but JACKIE flails herself free from TAMARA's embrace.)

JACKIE: Yes, I know I'm absholutely pished, piddled and newted, but still it's no! And I just can't be doing with this *'Night on a Nude Mountain'.*

(She switches the gramophone off.)

TAMARA: It's *Night on a 'Bare' Mountain* actually, Sweet Lips.

JACKIE: Who wrote it, anyhow? Rimshkykorokoff, or Ripphercorsetsoff! Well, it was certainly Rippingsomething-or-other-off!

TAMARA: No, it was Moussorgsky. Rimsky only arranged it.

(JANE re-appears with an open wine bottle. As JANE pours herself a glass, the now ashen-faced JACKIE hugs the Panda to her stomach.)

JACKIE: Oh dearie, dearie me! I think I'm going for a Technicoloured yawn. Where's the bathroom?

(She staggers to the window holding the Panda, but quickly JANE guides her to the stairs.)

JANE: Now remember, darling, you've got to climb several jumping-blocks called 'stairs', so carefully does it.

JACKIE: Oh, Janey, don't be such a shilly-billy!

(JANE watches JACKIE attempt to climb the stairs as the girl disappears from the Audience's view. But JACKIE only manages

about five stairs. Then we hear five distinct bumps as JACKIE topples down them.

A moment later JACKIE's head appears around the door. She is on her hands and knees.)

JACKIE: Yeah, you're right; there are blocks of shtairs that jump. Lots of 'em. Ugh, I do feel really pukey. Come on, Humphy. Together we're going to shprawl… I mean, crawl…up them jumping shtairs…

(JACKIE exits on her hands and knees with the Panda, and this time she is successful in her ascent. JANE closes the door.)

TAMARA: She is a truly…succulent child. I could eat her – alive.

JANE: Don't you dare!

TAMARA: Why? Are you jealous, my sweeting?

JANE: She's not for you.

TAMARA: Why don't you rant at me? Tell me what a lascivious blood-sucker I am.

JANE: 'Cause it would only encourage you to be even worse. Speaking of which; have you prepared the candles?

TAMARA: Please.

JANE: Please, Tamara – have you prepared the candles?

TAMARA: They're on the table in the passageway. Get them.

(JANE goes into the passageway, and returns with some tall black candles.)

JACKIE: Joseph should've rung by now. Well, it's nearly a quarter past one, for God's sake. He's never as late as this. 'Fact he's always on time in bed. When he can manage to do it, that is. Which is not as often as I'd like.

(TAMARA watches JANE arrange the black candles on the crimson table cloth by the black-draped window.)

TAMARA: Are you trying to offend me, Babykins? Talking about your ride-a-cock stallion like that? Do you want to put such a sexual strain on my digestive juices that I detonate and explode?

JANE: No, 'cause then there'll be everyone's blood everywhere.

TAMARA: Yes, but seriously, Sugarpuff. Does that gorgeous child know about our menage-a-deux? Has the outs and ins of us sunk through her A-cup-bra yet? And... *(showing her teeth.)* ...more to the point, does she know what we're going to do to you know who? *(TAMARA lets out a sudden blood-curdling cry as she pulls a handkerchief from her pocket and covers her nose with it.)* Oh not another sanguinary nasal haemorrhage!

(TAMARA rushes out of the room and clambers up the stairs. JANE watches TAMARA exit with a certain amount of disgust. Then she pours herself some more wine, and calls out to WOLFY, her pussy-dog.)

JANE: Wolfy! Dearest Wolfy! Come to Daddy. Ah, there you are... you lovely Pussy-dog. *(She mimes taking the pussy-dog into her arms and stroking it, and we realise for the first time in the play that the pussy-dog is imaginary. She continues to stroke it as she talks to it.)* There's nothing better, is there? – than you snuggling up to me like this. Yes, I'm a real silly-billy, aren't I? – to drink so much. Mind, you're such a greedy pussy-doggy, 'cause you smell like a kitty-litter factory. But I've called you now, doggy-pussy, 'cause I need your advice. So what d'you think would happen, Wolfy, if a juicy bundle of female flesh was found among the foaming rocks, with nothing on but her fur coat and tiara? In other words she'd be discovered in all her natural beauty; i.e., with rouged cheeks, fluorescent lipstick, false eyelashes, false hair-piece and... *(Stroking her own breasts.)* ...falsies. And no one would ever know that she accidentally tripped over *you* on the beach and smashed her head on a rock, and then she was swept out to sea. Accidental death from drowning would be the verdict. Then only you and I would remember her cruelty – which is like a wisdom tooth screaming through the meshes of my gums. But to the rest of the world, she'd merely be just another shattered beauty that was a plaything of the sea, while an army of seagulls pecked out her eyes. And she doesn't know how close those beaks are now, does she, Wolfy? Poor Fangers. Yes Tammers, you'd better be careful you don't bite off more than you can chew with those lovely incisors of yours. *(The telephone rings. Tentatively she picks up the receiver.)* Hythe 1812?... Oh, it's only you... Well, it could have been the Queen again, asking for your resignation... You've been drinking!... We're not talking about *me*, we're talking about *you*... Yes, I *am* in bed. With Tammers... *(Laughing.)* You don't think that's funny. Pity... So you'll be home in a few minutes. Good. Then we can get on with...

(TAMARA has entered halfway through the telephone conversation. But JANE only becomes aware of her when TAMARA takes the phone away from her. Then TAMARA finishes JANE's sentence for her into the receiver.)

TAMARA: ...The ecstasy and the chopped diamonds, Joseph. 'Cause the arsenic obviously hasn't taken root yet in your abdomen, but it will. Mind, you're such a lovely, hysterical man that – given half the chance – I bet you can do the most erogenous things with your big toes. Ooooh... *(She looks at the receiver curiously, and then hangs up.)* He hung up on me. Funny man. But then most funny men are. And it sounded like the poor Joe-Schmo was blubbering. Wonder why. We haven't even begun yet.

JANE: *(Pointedly downing another glass of wine.)* So close to being savaged by seagulls, eh, Wolfy. But shall we stop her before it all splurges round me? Shall I?

(In response TAMARA grabs JANE by the hair. Then she forces JANE to look into her eyes.)

TAMARA: It's too late for that. But then you always leave things too late. Especially as this is the interlude before the firework display. Now don't suck your thumb. Sometimes you're such a slimy mess.

JANE: *(Breaking away from her.)* Tamara, I don't think I can go through with it. I really don't!

TAMARA: If you fail us, I'll tell him everything.

JANE: *(Whimpering.)* Where's Humphy? Where's my Panda bear gone?

TAMARA: Humphy's all snuggled up between Jackie's budding breasts and pawing at her maidenhead.

JANE: *(After swigging some wine.)* Why must you always be so…?

TAMARA: *(Finishing her sentence.)* …Truthful! Because I need you to remember the Ladies' Rooms and the ornate boudoirs where you used to adore doing the spicy things we did. But now you've gone all soft and soppy on me. *(She presses her forefinger against JANE's forehead.)* You don't apply *that* anymore. Instead you now think with the urge of your blubbery breasts and your womb. Whereas a year ago you had a real body. Like a young Goddess.

JANE: How can you be so relentlessly horrid? I wore these incredibly tight jeans today just for you.

TAMARA: *(Squeezing JANE's waistline.)* But they don't hide the blancmange. The jelly fish.

JANE: *(Breaking away from her.)* For God's sake, just leave me alone, will you?

(TAMARA grabs JANE by the shoulders and forces her to sit down by the table.)

TAMARA: Don't move! We're about to begin. Now concentrate, and repeat over in your mind what I say to you.

JANE: But…

TAMARA: *(Silencing JANE with a stern finger over her lips.)* Now repeat; man is unnecessary. That is why we've been planning this endurance test for him. And them. All of them. Long before you ever met him. Because we women are the pain bearers, and we suffer for them continuous humiliation. We're the ones who sweat, honour and obey under the bucking eiderdowns, on our backs or our faces, to give pleasure to these self-satisfied, sadistic centaurs. *(Sensuously she strokes JANE's neck and shoulders.)* Yes, and we shave off the natural glories from our armpits. For them. We pluck out the offending hairs from our eyebrows. For them. We sit in steaming hair-saloons for hours merely to acquire fifteen-and-six, frizzed beehive hair-dos on top of our aching heads. Just for them. Then we stumble out into Man's air on a Man's street, sporting our blonde peroxide and false nails, wearing high heels that rape our feet and breed in-growing nails. For them. Indeed, our toes are only allowed out of our crippling shoes under a man's table, when the man is guzzling and pigging his food with one hand, whilst he's drunkenly groping our stockinged knees with his other sticky claw. And we endure all this wall-to-wall, humiliating serfdom just for them. Yes, since the first putrid kiss in old Eden Park, when the gutsing of the apple loosed the Man's Serpent into the world, the Serpent has continued to spurt his unwanted sperm from his pink phallus into our enslaved wombs. *(She pulls back the black drapes from the window/French doors to reveal a moonlit seascape.)* And so we women are now like millions and millions of sea animals that aimlessly ooze under the moon-washed waves.

JANE: Oh God help us!

TAMARA: He won't, 'cause the Old Bastard's male! So come with me – because *I* will help you, and free you. *(She takes JANE by the hand and leads her to the window. TAMARA opens the French doors. We hear the waves pounding the beach. JANE slumps down by the window, with her arms around a comforting cushion. Within a few moments JANE has fallen into a drunken sleep. But*

TAMARA is so wrapped up in her own vision, she doesn't notice that she is talking to herself.) Now listen, baby…listen! And you will hear the creatures of the sea flexing their slimy tendrils between the clashing waves. Because like us, they, too, are waiting to limpet themselves onto the narcissistic male-whale's back and the arrogant barracuda. Then they'll gnaw through the whale's blubber and prise open the ribcage of the barracuda. And then, together, we will feed on their bestial hearts like trillions of octopus cancers! *(She looks down at JANE, and realises that JANE is snoring.)* You've deteriorated into a weak woman again, who can do nothing but snore like a sow! *(She kneels beside JANE and squeezes her snoring nose. JANE wakes up, panting for air and half choking.)* Jane! You don't want me to really deal with you, do you?

JANE: *(Stumbling away from TAMARA.)* No! Please don't, Tamara. I beg you…

TAMARA: You've just committed an act of sedition.

JANE: How?

TAMARA: You went to sleep when I was talking. And that is treasonable, you ungrateful bitch. Especially as our beast will materialise here at any moment.

JANE: I'm very sorry, but I can't go through with it. See, I realise, Tamara – that despite everything – well, I still love him. We've been married for a whole year and half now, and there's been more good than bad. And I've found some peace – wrapped up in his 'jama jacket. He's got such a nice, cuddly 'jama jacket. And cute, cuddly, candy-striped 'jama trousers. And we have the same bitter-sweet taste in our mouths in the morning. So, on the whole, Joseph's been quite good to me. For a man, that is. No threats, or frenzy. And, above all, he does respect me. And *you* rarely respect me. Yes, and I doubt you ever will again!

TAMARA: *(Twisting JANE's ear – semi-playfully.)* You'll only get my respect back when *you* regain your lost power. And you will! *(Pinching JANE's waistline.)* Because under all your newly-acquired blancmange, there is still the same old bitter gripings that you've always felt about men. About the way they've habitually treated you. So men have got to pay in kind. Well, have I trained you for nothing? Put up with your ridiculous loneliness and inner despair for nothing? So stop lying to yourself. You've loved all the rubber and wetness and bondage, and everything we did together. And when this is over, we'll do it again and again and again until you die screaming in ecstasy!

(With her fingers tangled in JANE's hair, TAMARA yanks JANE's head back. Then she kisses JANE passionately. JANE fights her away free, waving her arms to hold TAMARA at bay.)

JANE: If you do that again, I'll scream the bloody place down!

(TAMARA crosses to her, and gazes into JANE's eyes.)

TAMARA: Janey…you know I'll never leave you. Wherever you go, and whoever you try to hide behind, rely on it, I will always be there. *With* you. And *for* you. And part of you. As, equally, you will always be part of me. So stop looking for tragedy in things. It doesn't exist. All that exists is the on-going rottenness of men. Therefore you must do everything we've rehearsed. Then, believe me, you will see what the little turd is really made of. And I can see from your eyes…that now you *do* believe me. So finish what you were doing – while I go and prepare for the Alien.

(TAMARA exits through the Stage Left door into the garden. In stunned silence JANE gazes after her. As if in a trance, ritualistically JANE draws the black drapes over the window. Then she lights the black candles on the black table.

She is about to leave the room, when she trips over something that we cannot see by the desk, and falls flat on her face.)

JANE: You stupid, bloody Pussy-Dog! Why didn't you get out of my way? Especially as you're supposed to be dead. *(She gets to her feet, and kicks the invisible animal out through the open French doors.)* Now go on, Wolfy, get out of here!

And stay out, or I'll murder *you*, too! *(She is about to shut the French doors.)* No, better leave them open. Perhaps she's right; perhaps the sea is about to possess the land – and we don't need men anymore. Except to grovel slavishly at our feet. *(She leaves the French doors open, but she closes the black drapes again.)* But there's still definitely something wrong in the way the world turns. *(Off, there is the sound of a door slamming.)* Ah…the Iceman cometh.

(Off, we hear a lot of cursing and a clatter of stumbling feet. The Stage Left door swings open and JOSEPH stumbles in with his briefcase. He is slightly tipsy. He takes no notice of JANE as he kicks off his shoes.)

JOSEPH: Christ. What a mess! My feet are on fire. What a godawful mess.

JANE: *(Handing him a drink.)* Hello.

JOSEPH: Thought you were in bed. *(Drinking.)* With Fangers.

JANE: I was.

JOSEPH: You're pissed.

JANE: Snap.

JOSEPH: So where is old Sexy Nose-Bleed?

JANE: Gone. She said the experiment wouldn't work. So she flew away.

JOSEPH: That's the only snippet of good news I've had all night. *(Pulling his socks off and massaging his feet.)* 'Specially as bits of my feet keep flaking off. Important bits. Toes and things. *(Downing the rest of his glass.)* Buggeration!

JANE: *(Undoing his tie for him.)* Now relax, darling, relax. Tell me what happened – and then relax.

(She takes off his suit jacket, and helps him on with his velvet smoking jacket.)

JOSEPH: Well, I gave the Minister all the encouraging words I could come up with. Millions of 'em. And half of I didn't understand, so I knew he was clueless. *(She pours him another drink which he swigs back.)* The Minister just glazed his eyes at me. As always, he looked fat, green and slimy like a ginormous bullfrog about to burst. And all the time he kept on taking phone call after phone call from China and India. Apparently Mao Tse Tung – who the Minister calls 'Old Lychee Face' – well, Mao is seriously thinking about taking his pissed-and-now-deceased Ambassador at his word, and so Mao will probably declare war on India in the morning. Then while we're having our Saturday fry-up, there'll be millions and millions of lychees having a go at millions and millions of mangoes. And as the Minister realised the horrendous import of this, I watched his cheekbones widen, his eyes go all slanty while his general pudge took on a genuine Oriental jaundiced hue. 'Fact the Minister began to look just like Huang Chang Ho, the Chinese Ambassador. The only thing that disappointed me was – unlike the Chinese Ambassador – the old Bullfrog didn't throw up over my pinstripes and drop dead! So God knows what's going to happen to any of us. Let's hope it'll all be different in the morning. Perhaps I'll be different, too…

JANE: I love you, Joe. I'm telling you now – for what it's worth. You see, I'm not like her. Not really. *(She undoes her shirt. She is wearing a black bra.)* Would you like to?

JOSEPH: What?

JANE: Study me. In your study.

JOSEPH: *(Gently pulling her towards him.)* Absolutely.

JOSEPH: Then sit on the table. *(She does so.)* You're so lovely. *(He lies on the table, with his head in her lap.)* Don't worry, darling…I'll bring your usual Sunday fry-up to you in bed in the morning.

(He pretends to snore.)

JANE: *(Laughing affectionately.)* Oh you old softy. *(Stroking his chin.)* Ugh, you need a shave. It's all your wickedness trying to get out. *(He growls in what he regards as a sexy manner.)* We've got another visitor, you know, so we might as well go to bed.

JOSEPH: *(Jumping off the table.)* Not another fornicating visitor! Oh Humph! I can't go on. It's worse than being married to Mary.

JANE: *(Trying to undo his shirt buttons.)* But, if you like, first we can have rumpy-pumpy on your desk.

JOSEPH: *(Backing away from her.)* Who the hell is this frigging visitor?!

(As if on cue, the Stage Right door opens, and a WOMAN, with a red beehive hair-do, appears in the doorway. She is in her mid-thirties, over-made-up, dressed in a mini-skirt and an imitation mink coat, and she is wearing ginormous ear-rings. She speaks with a pronounced Northern accent.)

WOMAN: *(To JOSEPH.)* You are, luv.

JOSEPH: *(Open-mouthed.)* Mary! Mary!

WOMAN: Was a little lamb, luv. And quite contrary.

JOSEPH: But it can't be you, Mary, 'cause you're…well, you're dead! Or at least you should be.

(Laughing the WOMAN slips through the black drapes that are covering the French door, and disappears out into the night. In fear and amazement JOSEPH turns to JANE for some response.)

JANE: You look as if you've scene a ghost, dear.

JOSEPH: I bloody have!

(Then yelling, 'Mary! Mary!' like a demented banshee, JOSEPH fights his way through the black drapes, and runs out into the night in pursuit of the WOMAN.

JANE pours herself another drink and smiles tiredly.

Moments later JOSEPH re-enters through the black drapes.)

JOSEPH: What the hell is going on here? That couldn't be Mary. Couldn't be! *(With his head in hands.)* I must've drunk so much, I'm seeing things!

JANE: *(Imitating MARY's Northern accent.)* It's a game, luv. So you'd best join in – while you still can, luv.

JOSEPH: *(Pouring himself a drink.)* A glass or two of this port is what I need. This'll sober me up. 'Cause I intend to get to the bottom of this. And for starters… *(After swigging back the port.)* …what, in the Devil's name, are those bloody black drapes and the Satanic black candles for?

JANE: You're a 'devil' sight closer than you think. *(In her Northern accent.)* And – like I said, luv – it's a game which – like it or not – you have to play.

JOSEPH: No, Janey, don't push me. I've had a mawful of faeces already. So how did my wife get here?

JANE: You brought me here a year and a half ago.

JOSEPH: *(Shouting.)* My other wife!

JANE: Bigamist!

JOSEPH: My dead wife!

JANE: Murderer!

JOSEPH: It's a figure of speech!

JANE: Whose figure? *(Violently JOSEPH grabs her.)* Rapist! *(She tries to knee him the crotch, so he backs off. Then she buttons up her shirt.)* Yes, Tamara's been right all along. You spuming male-whales are all the same!

JOSEPH: Spuming male-whales?

JANE: Not to mention unwanted sperming serpents.

(At that moment the WOMAN re-enters through the French doors behind JOSEPH, catching him unawares. Then the WOMAN spins

JOSEPH round to face her, the WOMAN she kisses him full and long on the mouth. JOSEPH responds. Then shaking his head, he breaks away from her.)

JOSEPH: Yes…very, very, very nice. But it's nothing like the kiss that Mary could saliva up. So what's next? I'm so wasted it doesn't matter. Though I must admit, you really did fool me a moment ago.

(The WOMAN removes her red wig. It is TAMARA. Then TAMARA takes her face-cream out of her handbag, and swiftly removes her heavy makeup.)

TAMARA: Naturally. You're a man, so making a fool of you wasn't difficult.

JOSEPH: But why'd you dress up as my wife? *(JANE switches off the main light, leaving only the candlelight.)* And I can do without the shadows. *(To TAMARA who is fixing her face.)* So why did you pretend to be Mary?

TAMARA: To remind you of the things behind you. *(Nervously JOSEPH looks behind him.)* Oh not the shadows. Or the Chinese threat. No, it's all your personal history, Joseph – that you think you've buried. And which now you have to resurrect, and confront. Face to face.

JOSEPH: *(Laughing hysterically as he pours himself a drink.)* You're just another half-emancipated-over-sexed-not-getting-it-enough-two-breaster, aren't you?

(In response TAMARA closes her handbag, and picks up the large covered-object on the chair by the window. Then she places the object on the black tablecloth in the flickering candlelight.)

TAMARA: Uncover, and let there be light!

JOSEPH: No, not that!

JANE: *(Whipping the dust-cloth off the object with a dramatic flourish.)* Yes; hey presto, and all is revealed!

(We see that the object is the model of a cathedral, constructed of wood and glass. The cathedral is very beautiful as it glitters in the candlelight. JOSEPH falls to his knees in front of the cathedral, and puts his arms around it protectively.)

JOSEPH: People can let you down, but objects never will. You've no idea the wondrous hours I put into creating this.

TAMARA: Yes…and how exquisitely the stained-glass glistens in the candlelight. So – now allow me to lift the roof off your hidden Saviour.

JOSEPH: No, it's mine! I will. *(With great care he lifts the roof off the cathedral to reveal the pews, the golden altar and a glowing stained glass window.)* It took an eternity of boyhoods to make this. A woman's fingers could never have embroidered the unicorn entwined with the Christ on the altar cloth – like I did.

TAMARA: But you don't believe in Christ.

JOSEPH: I never said I did. It was just something to do with all the endless hours.

TAMARA: Yes, Mummy and Daddy never really loved you, did they? Although they did occasionally take you to Ireland in the holidays, to see the ancient ruins and all the nuns. Which were often interchangeable. But your parents only did this to remind you of the desolation that would enshroud you for the rest of your life.

JOSEPH: What my parents did is my concern! *(Swigging back his drink.)* Look, I can throw you out now. You know that.

TAMARA: But you won't.

JOSEPH: *(Pleading.)* Janey, for God's sake, support me. I mean, what kind of influence is she on…well, on Jackie?

TAMARA: Yes, Joey, you're hooked, alright. *(She strokes the cathedral's spire.)* How many fruitless hours did you spend trying to get this spire to stand straight, with all those innumerable tubes of aeroplane glue?

JOSEPH: Don't touch it!

TAMARA: *(Pointing.)* And although you don't believe, you still say your nocturnal prayers in front of the altar, don't you?

JOSEPH: I warn you – if you continue in this manner, Fanghorn, I shall be forced to insert my foot right up your frontal pivot!

(JACKIE appears in the Stage Right doorway, hugging her Panda bear. We hear bath-water running upstairs. The moment JOSEPH sees JACKIE, he moves in front of his cathedral to prevent his daughter seeing it.)

JACKIE: Good afternoon, everybody. Well, it is nearly two in the morning, isn't it? And all your hollering and ranting woke me up. But that's no bad thing 'cause now I've slept most of it off.

JOSEPH: Slept most of what off?

JACKIE: My drunk-as-a-skunkness. And I've wiped nearly all of my puke off Humphy. So he's come down for a goodnight kiss-and-cuddle.

(JACKIE thrusts the panda at JOSEPH, who thrusts the panda straight back at her.)

JOSEPH: He stinks! *(Gesturing towards the stairs.)* And what's that water running?

JACKIE: The bath. For Humphy.

JOSEPH: You can't bath a stuffed Panda bear. He'll end up as a mess of water-logged sog! Look, for pity's sake, do something, Janey. Take Jackie back up to bed, and then throw Miss Nose Bleed out! Or, preferably, vice-versa!

JANE: *(To JACKIE.)* Darling, when did you say you were going up to London to stay with Tamara?

JOSEPH: No, this is all far too much!

JANE: *(Shaking her head.)* Only costs a couple of pounds return.

JOSEPH: God in Hell!

TAMARA: That's probably where you'll find Him.

JOSEPH: Jackie, go back to bed this instant. And, when you're
up there, turn off that bleeding bath!

JACKIE: I don't have to, cause Granddad says he'll turn the
bath off when the water starts to come under his bedroom
door.

JOSEPH: *(Hysterically.)* A rose is a rose is a rose is a rose but
there's no need to turn it into a bleeding General Election!
Tamara! Janey! I appeal to your better senses. That's if you
have any! Please leave the child out of this!

JACKIE: What child?

JOSEPH: *(Wrapping JACKIE's arms tightly around the Panda.)* Now
you and Humphy – God, he stinks – go upstairs and have
a cuddle together, because your mother and I…

JACKIE: *(Overriding him.)* Step-mother.

JOSEPH: Step-mother and I are going to have a serious talk,
so…

TAMARA: *(Interrupting him.)* Jackie, did you know your father
was a failed architect?

JOSEPH: For mercy's sake, will you stop…?

JANE: *(Overriding him and pointing at the cathedral on the table.)*
Yes, and so instead of spending the time he should with
you, Jackie, he spends most of his spare moments sticking
pieces of glass onto bits of old wood.

JACKIE: Oh but your cathedral's so beautiful. No, it really is
beautiful, Daddy. Can I touch it? *(Dropping the Panda.)* Will
it break?

JOSEPH: Yes, of course, it'll break! And I'll show it to you
properly in the morning, but now it's time for you to…

JACKIE: *(Taking no notice of him as she carefully picks up the cathedral to look at it.)* It's absolutely super!

JOSEPH: *(Hovering and twitching.)* No, no, please put it back on the table, Jackie!

JACKIE: It is fantastic! You're such a clever Daddypops. And just look at these stained glass paintings.

(JACKIE sways gently with the cathedral in her arms. JOSEPH tries to take it from his daughter, but TAMARA restrains him.)

JOSEPH: Jackie, for Christ's sake!

TAMARA: If you jostle her, she's sure to drop it, 'cause she's been seriously on the piss.

JANE: Yes, we thought a proper piss-up would do her a world of good.

JOSEPH: You destructive bitches!

(Still clutching the cathedral, JACKIE begins a swaying dance in front of TAMARA.)

TAMARA: Look at those shadows behind you, Joseph. They're fornicating. *(Momentarily disorientated JOSEPH looks behind him for a second. As he turns his back, TAMARA puts out her foot, tripping JACKIE up. JACKIE drops the cathedral, which lands on a cushion, so it is not seriously damaged.)* Oh dear, it seems the shadows have just come to a climax.

JOSEPH: *(Apoplectically pushing JACKIE across the room.)* You drunken little tart!

TAMARA: That's a charming thing to say to your daughter.

(In his apoplectic frenzy JOSEPH snatches an épée from the wall, prompting JACKIE to cower behind the desk.)

JOSEPH: *(Whirling round on TAMARA with his épée.)* No, you're right, Fanghorn, because *you're* the one who's responsible for all this mayhem. *(He advances on TAMARA, who is not afraid and holds her ground.)* So now I'm going to winkle your eyes out and serve 'em to the cockles!

TAMARA: *(Smiling.)* But shellfish are not in season, dearie. At least not until there's an 'r' in the month.

JOSEPH: Stabbing's too good for you!

JACKIE: *(Coming out from behind the desk.)* Now stop it, both of you, stop it! What you're doing's just horrible! *(Going into her tipsy baby-talk routine.)* Janey, I need another little dwinkey now. Just a teeny-weeny dwop of dwinkey.

JANE: *(handing her the bottle.)* That's my girl.

JOSEPH: Yes, Tamara, I'm not going to stab you. 'Cause I've decided that the only way that you'll learn your humble place in my house, is if I undress you slowly with my épée. Yes, that will make you look even more absurd than you do already. Which'll take some doing.

TAMARA: *(Smiling.)* That'll really turn you on, won't it?

JOSEPH: I'm past caring. What's more, when you're naked, I might complete your humiliation by having you over my desk.

JANE: You whoremaster! Tammers was right. All you men are worse than animals. With your disgusting masculine smells, your sweat, your fly-buttons, sticky condoms, tobacco breath and your dirty underpants.

JOSEPH: *(Emptying his glass with one hand while he twirls his épée with the other.)* Say what you like, wifey. I'm too pissed to care. See, I'm still the master in this house. I'm Tom-Stud-Jones. And I fancy having my wicked way with Fang 'Horn'. Besides, you don't really care, Janey. I thought you did. But you're just as morally polluted as she is. You both need a joint bath in Dettol. *(To his daughter.)* So you'd better get back to bed, Jackie, now.

JACKIE: I'm not going anywhere. I don't want to miss your rumpy-pumpy. 'Cause when I tell my school mates what you lot get up to, I'll go straight to the top of the sex-scandal averages.

JOSEPH: Go to bed!

JACKIE: No!

JOSEPH: *(Pointing to his fallen cathedral on a cushion.)* Haven't you done enough?

JACKIE: No! 'Cause you care a bloody sight more about your rotten cathedral than you do about me.

JOSEPH: That's not true! Now go to bed.

JACKIE: No way, Hosé. If there's going to be any fun, I'm going to watch it. 'Fact I might even join in.

JOSEPH: *(Losing his temper and clipping JACKIE around the ear.)* Now take pukey Humphy and get yourself up to bed!

JANE: *(Flailing her arms at him.)* Joseph, that was unforgivable!

(JOSEPH stops JANE in her tracks by levelling his épée at her chest.)

JOSEPH: I will, Jane.

JANE: I believe you, Joseph.

JOSEPH: I never would have even thought about it before tonight but…

JACKIE: *(Weeping.)* You've really hurt my ear, Dad!

(JOSEPH tries to comfort JACKIE, but she shrugs him off.)

JOSEPH: Oh I'm sorry, darling, I didn't mean it…

TAMARA: *(Overriding him.)* Liar! You enjoyed it. You're so priapically obvious with your épées, your sabres and your foils. Talking of which; what about this?

(TAMARA slides open his desk drawer, and she pulls out a bullwhip. Then she slithers its thong along the desk.)

JOSEPH: How, in the name of Jesus, did you find that?

JACKIE: *(Tearfully cuddling the Panda bear.)* We don't love him anymore, do we, Humphy?

JOSEPH: Jackie, I really didn't mean to do that. You just exasperated me and…

(TAMARA silences him by cracking the whip. Then she tosses the whip back into the desk drawer.)

TAMARA: It's too late for apologies. You're on your way out.

JOSEPH: Yes, and I've had it up to here with all your shit!

(He lunges at TAMARA with his épée. Adroitly she weaves to one side, unhooks a sabre from the wall, and elegantly parries his sword-cut to her head. Then she lunges at JOSEPH, snicking his arm. Her fencing agility takes him by surprise, so initially he defends himself clumsily. Then he slashes at her legs. She jumps over his scything blade, and with an adroit flick of her wrist, she disarms him with her sabre.)

JOSEPH: That's ridiculous! You couldn't've possibly have done that. And you've twisted my handlebar moustache.

TAMARA: If that's all I've twisted, count yourself lucky.

(Dismissively she tosses her sabre down on the desk.)

JOSEPH: You crowing, cocky, catty, crapulous cow!

TAMARA: There's nothing like a mixed metaphor.

(With a frustrated roar, JOSEPH hurls himself at TAMARA, and attempts to strangle her. But again TAMARA is too agile for him. With a judo-twist of her wrist, she hurls him against his desk. Now half stunned JOSEPH shakes his head in utter disbelief.)

JOSEPH: You're bloody inhuman is what you are!

(TAMARA smiles, showing her teeth.)

TAMARA: Glad you've caught on.

(JOSEPH tries to straighten his handle-bar moustache with one hand while he rubs his painful head with other.)

JOSEPH: What in hell hit me?

TAMARA: Your desk.

(Warily JOSEPH gets to his feet. He circles around TAMARA, looking for an opening to attack. She watches him with an inviting smile. With a lion's roar, he charges at her. But she weaves to one side and trips him up. Simultaneously she slams the edge of her hand down onto the back of his neck. JOSEPH collapses on the carpet unconscious.

JACKIE pushes the gloating TAMARA away from her inert father. Then protectively she cradles him in her arms.)

JACKIE: You can't do things like that to my Daddy. You can't!

JANE: *(Apprehensively.)* You really mean it, Tamara, don't you?

TAMARA: Take his clothes off.

JACKIE: Oh come on, you can't take his clothes off. Can you? If you do…. *(She clambers to her feet and pours herself some more wine.)* …he'll be all nudies. Then he won't be my Daddy anymore, he'll just be a nudies man. But I suppose it doesn't matter, 'cause his undies are all holes. So then he'll be… *(Laughing and crying.)* …nothing but holey nudies, won't he?

TAMARA: Shut up.

JACKIE: I can say what I like. He's my Dad.

TAMARA: Yes, but I won't take you up to London with me, and you won't have new clothes, expensive dinners and other men 'nudies' if you don't put a sock in it. Talking of which, take his socks off, Jackie. And, Janey, you can divest him of his smoking jacket.

(Glowering JANE pulls his jacket off.)

JANE: Believe me, Tamara, you're very close to pushing me too far, and then…

TAMARA: *(Overriding her.)* Now remove the skunk's silk tie and shirt.

(JACKIE tugs off her father's second sock.)

JACKIE: Ugh! What niffy tootsies!

TAMARA: There's nothing like a preview of decomposition.

JACKIE: *(To TAMARA.)* What part of London do you live in?

TAMARA: Westminster Bridge.

JACKIE: I mean, *where* do you live?

TAMARA: Westminster Abbey. *I'll* take his trousers off.

(TAMARA starts to undo his trouser belt.)

JANE: You want him, don't you? Just because I've had him. You're thirsting to taste what I've tasted. Yes, for once, you might even like a bit of rough.

TAMARA: Shut it!

JANE: It could even add another dimension to you – like femininity.

(Frenziedly TAMARA yanks JOSEPH's trousers off, so now JOSEPH is naked but for his briefs.)

TAMARA: Rip the telephone out.

JANE: I can hear the seagulls screeching for eyeballs.

TAMARA: Do it! *(JANE pulls the telephone lead out from the points at the wall.)* Now tie his feet up with the lead.

JACKIE: I can't tie him up, he's my Daddy.

(TAMARA glowers at JACKIE, who immediately goes silent.)

JANE: Hadn't I better get some pliers to cut the phone from the flex?

TAMARA: No. The poor dumbdumb might want to ring up the P.M. with his big toe.

(FANGHORN laughs hysterically, which makes JACKIE cry as she cuddles her Panda bear.)

JACKIE: Boohoo, boohoo! What's there to laugh at, Humphy? When it's all so horrible.

(JANE finishes tying up JOSEPH's feet, while TAMARA ties his hands behind his back with his trouser belt.)

TAMARA: Oh come on, Jackie, stop trying to seduce Humph, and help us lift this fossilised turd onto the table. Take hold of his feet.

(Tearfully JACKIE obeys, while TAMARA and JANE lift JOSEPH up by his shoulders. Then together the three of them lug JOSEPH onto the table, with his feet Down Stage. TAMARA props his head up with some cushions, so that the Audience can see his face.)

JACKIE: I'll kill you both if you hurt Daddy anymore! I really will.

(TAMARA places two flickering black candles behind JOSEPH's head, and two candles at his feet. TAMARA shouts up the stairs.)

TAMARA: Grandpussy, get your idle ass down here! We need you.

GRANDPA: *(Off, shouting back.)* But I haven't finished mopping up me bleeding bedroom floor!

TAMARA: You incontinent old codger! Couldn't you wait 'till you got to the bathroom?

GRANDPA: *(Off, as we hear him thundering down the stairs.)* It's tap-water I'm mopping up, not me pissing piddle!

(GRANDPA's furious face appears in the doorway.)

JACKIE: Didn't you turn my bath off, then, Grandpa?

GRANDPA: Suffering poltergeists! I wondered why me bed was floating.

JACKIE: Then go back up and turn the bath-tap off, for God's sake!

GRANDPA: I'm nothing but the general pussy-dog's body round here, ent I? Where is Wolfy, anyway?

(GRANDPA runs back upstairs.)

TAMARA: *(Shouting after him.)* There's no hurry, Grandpappy. No one cares if the Alien's ceiling comes in. 'Cause he's only a thing, with swinish trotters, a carrot nose and strawberry blobs for cheeks.

GRANDPA: *(Off.)* Where'd you say you've hidden all the carrots and strawberries? 'Cause I'm still absolutely ravenous. But I have switched off the bath. Yet hold on. It's still utter chaos up here! *(Still shouting GRANDPA thunders down the stairs again, carrying something that the Audience can't see.)* No, you should really see it up there. Joseph's bath-toys have gone berserk. His battle-ships and submarines are floating all round the floor. And his rubber Mickey Mouse has gone AWOL. Shall I try to bail the bathroom out with his plastic potty? *(As he produces JOSEPH's bright-pink plastic potty from behind his back, for the first time he sees the unconscious JOSEPH on the table.)* What the pigging-hell's going on here? *(He grins ravenously.)* Are you going to eat him? Look, I'm not against eating him, y'understand. I'm so hungry, I could even turn cannibal.

JANE: Jackie, for pity's sake, go upstairs and check how bad the damage really is.

JACKIE: Alright, I will. But you be good to my Dad while I'm gone, or I'll set the Police on the lot of you!

(JACKIE exits, running up the stairs.)

GRANDPA: So what the Devil's going on here? *(Pinching JOSEPH's exposed thigh.)* Experiments are all very well, but there's no need for wholesale obscenity by candlelight.

JACKIE: *(Off, shouting.)* It's not that bad up here! Yes, the bath has overflowed a bit, but I can easily mop it up. Grandpa's been exaggerating, as per bloody usual.

GRANDPA: *(To TAMARA.)* So what you going to do to me, then?

TAMARA: That depends on you.

GRANDPA: Hey, Janey! You're not going to stand there and watch this torturing trollop mess me about, are you?

JANE: *(Sitting on the table.)* No, I'm going to sit down and watch this torturing trollop mess you about. See, you've had much too much of your own way for much too long.

TAMARA: But if you do as you're told, you unnecessary bunch of tripe, there is a remote chance you'll live to see another night. But if not…

(TAMARA pulls the bullwhip out of the desk drawer and advances on GRANDPA. JANE grabs TAMARA's raised wrist.)

JANE: Anything but that!

GRANDPA: *(Cowering.)* She's right, Fangers, she's right! Look, whatever you want me to do, I'll do it! I'll even start washing my teeth from now on, and I'll sleep in the dark, and I won't play tiddly-winks with my fly-buttons or fart in the Cornflakes!

JANE: We've no wish to change your daily routines, Dad. Just be a good boy, and do exactly as you're told.

TAMARA: Yes, so go this instant, Gramps, and fetch your cut-throat razor.

GRANDPA: I've lost it. Ever since I stopped shaving my armpits for Lent.

TAMARA: *(Raising her whip.)* Cut-throat!

GRANDPA: *Yours* will get cut, Fangers, if you don't watch it. *(Calling towards the French doors.)* Wolfy! Wolfy! *(Indicating TAMARA.)* Even though you're dead, come and bite the tits off this rapacious flagellant.

TAMARA: Whatever is this…absurd, non-existent pussy-dog that you're all always on about? I've never seen her or him!

(GRANDPA opens the French windows and lets WOLFY in.)

GRANDPA: And you never will see Wolfy. 'Cause you have to believe, Fangers, and you don't. *(To WOLFY.)* Now in you come, my little lady-man. He's a nice pussy, isn't she? And he-she makes a noise between a growl and a purr, so I've nicknamed it 'Growl-Purr'. But don't stroke him, or she'll have your hand off.

TAMARA: *(Taking a gigantic kick at WOLFY.)* I can't bear cats!

GRANDPA: *(Picking WOLFY up and stroking him.)* He's a Doggy, aren't you, Pussy? You missed Wolfy, anyroad.

TAMARA: Enough. *(She cracks her bullwhip at GRANDPA.)* So go and fetch your cut-throat now. Or I'll cut yours!

(Hastily GRANDPA beats a retreat towards the stairs, muttering to himself.)

GRANDPA: Yes, we hate her, Wolfy, don't we? *(As he disappears up the stairs.)* But we'll be revenged on the whole pack of her!

JANE: *(Tentatively to TAMARA.)* So are you really going to do what you said you were going to do?

TAMARA: Watch and see. It will certainly have its moments.

(JACKIE re-appears, clutching her Panda bear.)

JACKIE: It's worse than I thought. The bathroom's ruined. 'Fact it needs to be seen to be believed.

TAMARA: Most things do. But don't worry, Jackie, my lovely, you're coming to London with me tomorrow.

JACKIE: I don't think I fancy it.

TAMARA: Now I want you to watch something.

JACKIE: Is it rude, or crude, or anything?

(GRANDPA runs in, with his cut-throat razor.)

GRANDPA: *(To TAMARA.)* You're not really going to do anything terrible, are you? God, I'm so dreadfully hungry.

(TAMARA takes the razor from GRANDPA. Simultaneously she pulls the roses out of the vase and places them in a pattern around JOSEPH's body. Then she pours the water from the vase over JOSEPH's face, and waves the razor at him.)

TAMARA: Wake up, babykins. It's morning time.

JANE: *(Rushing to defend JOSEPH.)* You can't! No, you can't!

(JOSEPH splutters back to consciousness.)

JOSEPH: No, I can't breathe, I can't…!

(TAMARA raises the cut-throat razor above her head as she addresses the still-spluttering JOSEPH.)

TAMARA: Now I'm going to cut off that part of you that offends me most!

(JACKIE faints.)

JOSEPH: *(Still spluttering.)* I don't understand what's going on…

TAMARA: You will.

GRANDPA: You can't!

JANE: The seagulls are coming.

TAMARA: RIGHT OFF!!!!

(As the cut-throat razor swoops down, there is an instant BLACKOUT.)

END OF ACT ONE

ACT TWO

As the Lights come up, there is a short cry, then we see TAMARA, with the raised cut-throat razor in one hand while triumphantly she holds aloft an unknown object in her other hand.

JOSEPH's body is hidden behind JANE and GRANDPA.

TAMARA: I have cut off that part of him that offended me most. *(She steps back from her victim. JANE props JOSEPH's head up as TAMARA illuminates his face with a candle. Then we see that his…handlebar moustache has been cut off! GRANDPA and JANE begin to laugh hysterically, and TAMARA joins in.)* Give the poor bozo a mirror. *(Laughing JANE thrusts a mirror in front of JOSEPH's uncomprehending face. TAMARA folds up her cut-throat razor and pockets it. Then she points to the unconscious JACKIE.)* Now wake her up.

(GRANDPA shakes JACKIE awake.)

JACKIE: *(Still fuzzy-headed and not daring to look at her father.)* I can't bear it! She didn't cut his…off! *(To TAMARA.)* Did you? *(TAMARA laughs. JACKIE clambers to her feet to look at her father.)* His moustache! You only cut off his beautiful moustache!

(JACKIE joins in the laughing with GRANDPA, JANE and TAMARA, but JACKIE's laughter borders on hysteria. Finally JANE shakes JOSEPH back into full consciousness. Then she makes him look in the mirror.)

JOSEPH: Oh no, I've been raped! *(He starts to cry.)* I would have preferred you to have cut off my donger than my handlebars!

(TAMARA fondles her bullwhip.)

JOSEPH: Now your nasal virility's gone, there's only the flaying of your flesh left. It's your so-called 'manly' pride that I want to strip off you.

JOSEPH: *(Sitting up.)* You're being a bit obvious, Fangers, aren't you? I expected something a little more subtle than moustache-circumcision followed by fallacious flagellation.

(TAMARA cracks her whip.)

JACKIE: No, you can't whip him, Tammers! If you try, I'll scratch your eyes out. And I don't want to go to London with you. I want to stay here with my Daddy, 'cause I love my Daddy.

TAMARA: *(To JACKIE.)* Yes, and your Daddy loves being beaten. Don't you, Joseph? Well, you loved your father beating you.

JOSEPH: My father never beat me!

TAMARA: Methinks the lady doth protest too much.

JANE: No, it's the truth, Tamara. Both his parents loved him. He's told me so many, many times.

TAMARA: And you really believe all the lies he tells you? *(TAMARA places the cathedral in the middle of the desk. Then she kneels in front of the cathedral, crosses herself and chants.)* In the name of the Father, the Son and the Holy Ghost. *(pronouncing it like 'Amen'.)* Ah…woman. *(She stands, confronting him. .)* But the only good thing your father ever did for you was he took you to your local church every Sunday. Then he led you up to the old weather-beaten church door because you were such a jolly little choirboy.

JOSEPH: That's a load of impious pillock!

(TAMARA opens a photograph album from the pile she brought with her when she first arrived. Then she thrusts the album under JOSEPH's nose.)

TAMARA: Lovely photo of you in your purple cassock, isn't it?

JOSEPH: You forged it! *(Hysterically.)* And there's that thing sitting in your eyes again, so would you kindly tell it to stand up while I'm talking?!

TAMARA: *(Discarding the album on the pile.)* But your father never went into the church with you, did he? Wonder why…

JOSEPH: *(Involuntarily blurting out.)* He couldn't bear the smell of incense! *(realising what he's said.)* What I mean is…

TAMARA: *(Triumphantly.)* Exactly!

JOSEPH: So what?! He said incense smelt like setting autumn on fire. What's that prove? Other than some people don't like smelling autumn on fire.

TAMARA: But *you* do, 'cause you love the stench of incense.

JOSEPH: Not on my chop suey and garlic salad, I don't!

TAMARA: Sunday after Sunday, with the incense lapping round you, you sat hunched up in the choir-stalls, as the Vicar dispensed his wafers of bread and translucent wine in the candlelight, while you went on reading your *Batman* and playing with yourself.

JOSEPH: That's just more litigious filth.

TAMARA: And as you sat there in the stalls, you wished that your father was Jesus Christ – i.e.; on the cross – and permanently nailed-up!

(With a wolf-like howl, JOSEPH snaps his bonds effortlessly and leaps off the table. Then he jumps into his trousers and wrenches his shirt back on. TAMARA watches unmoved.)

JOSEPH: I could've done that ages ago!

TAMARA: I know. I tied you loosely on purpose because I wanted to smell your Achilles heels.

JOSEPH: *(Now frantically buttoning his shirt.)* I'm getting out of here! This is a complete nut-house!

JACKIE: *(Throwing her arms around her father.)* Oh Daddy, Daddy! You look so funny and very silly without your waxed handlebars.

GRANDPA: Yes, and I've been silent long enough. I'm
so bleeding hungry, me stomach's about to implode.
(Clutching his abdomen.) It's like one big inverted belch
down here. So let's call it a night because the bathroom's
a swimming-pool. *(He picks up the strands of JOSEPH's
moustache.)* And this place is a barber's-shop, 'cause now
I've got bits of his moustache in me ears, up me nose and
in me codpiece.

JOSEPH: The dead in the lettuce-patch, Grandpus. And this is
as good as any time to remember them.

TAMARA: *(Smiling and showing her teeth.)* Trying to turn the
game round now, are you?

JOSEPH: Unlike you, Fanghorn, I don't play games. I'm
genuinely fascinated by decomposition. *(Putting on his
smoking jacket.)* And the old man knows exactly what I
mean.

GRANDPA: *(Frightened.)* But I'll never tell, Joseph! If you'll just
give me a sparrow's crumb to quiet my growling guttage.

TAMARA: There's nothing you can tell us, Grandpa, 'cause
your son-in-law's stuffed with lies from arsehole to
Christmas time. See, the truth is, he came from absolutely
nothing. All his stories about Eton and holidays in Ireland
with its old ruins and even older nuns, well, they're just
grandiloquent falsehoods. And the only place he could get
away from his sadistic Daddy was to retreat to his little
church on the hill.

JANE: But that's all blatantly untrue! For God's sake, tell her
she's wrong, Joseph!

TAMARA: So why does he keep a bullwhip in his desk and all
these swords in his armoury? And why does he wake up
screaming?

JANE: He suffers from lots of nightmares.

TAMARA: Right! And he screams because his father possesses him in his sleep.

JOSEPH: That's bilious bilge!

JACKIE: Well, I can't take anymore. I'm going to bed.

TAMARA: Do so, but you'll come back when I need you.

JACKIE: *(Kissing her father.)* Please, all of you, be good while I'm gone. At least try to be good.

(JACKIE exits.)

JANE: Is any of this true about your father, Joseph?

JOSEPH: I'm off to bed, too. But before I go, Fanghorn, I'm going to phone the Police, and have you taken away as a breaking-and-entering maniac. So you'll get three years' imprisonment for this night's work. 'Cause not only have you terrified and inebriated my daughter, who's under age, but also you've physically attacked me and vandalised my house. Not to mention performing Satanic rites on Grandpa's table, where you sexually assaulted my legendary moustache.

TAMARA: Janey, give him the telephone.

(JANE obeys.)

JOSEPH: Thank you. *(He dials without realising that the phone is disconnected.)* Funny...there's no dialling tone. *(Then he notices that it is disconnected.)* I see. Well, a little stroll down to the Police station will complete my sobering-up. *(He threads his trouser belt back on.)* I won't be long.

TAMARA: Strange death your father had.

JOSEPH: *(Turning apprehensively to face her.)* What d'you mean?

TAMARA: A shelf of exquisite glass.

JOSEPH: How'd you know...?

(He trails off.)

TAMARA: Aren't you bored with that question? Especially with those Florentine Bell champagne glasses, and eight cut-glass decanters with crystal stoppers.

JOSEPH: Alright, alright! So Father polished them every Godforsaken night of the week until they shone like millions of baby diamonds. So bleeding what?

GRANDPA: I'm still bleeding starving. That's bleeding what!

JANE: Joseph, you said your father was a… What did you say your father was?

JOSEPH: I didn't, but take him for all in all – he was a man. And night after night he used to fondle those crystal glasses like I would a woman. But it was sickening how those glasses were far more important to him than….

(JOSEPH trails off. Then abruptly he blows out the candles on the cathedral's miniature altar.)

TAMARA: And that's one of the many reasons your mother left him.

JOSEPH: Why are you so consumed with other people's lives, Fangers?

TAMARA: One Thursday afternoon, wasn't it? When you came home from school, there was a note on the table. Mum had left home for good, to shack up with another woman.

JOSEPH: And bloody good riddance, I say. She was no good, either. But I got him. I smashed his glasses up. And his decanters. And even the stoppers.

JANE: Why haven't you told me any of this before?

TAMARA: Then Daddy came home, didn't he? And when he saw all his shattered crystal, he took his bullwhip out of his desk drawer. *(She flexes the whip.)* Then he beat you 'till your blood leapt out of your flesh like a shoal of terrified salmon.

(She cracks the whip.)

JOSEPH: *(Trying to hide his fear of the whip.)* What nonsense!
You're making it all up.

TAMARA: Yes...and like your father, I, too, am an expert with
a bullwhip. And the whip frightens you, doesn't it? I've
spent weeks studying what frightens you.

JOSEPH: Alright, you've made your point, so put it away.
Please...I'm asking you nicely.

TAMARA: *(placing the whip on the desk.)* Yes... and now this
whip is lying by itself on your desk – even though it's
still coiled like a sleeping boa constrictor – yet it seems
completely harmless, doesn't it? And, indeed, it would
have lain like this for centuries, itching for flesh. Waiting.
Until that day your father grasped it.

JOSEPH: Please, just leave it asleep where it is! I beg you.

TAMARA: Confess, then. Confess.

JOSEPH: To what?

TAMARA: *(Lifting the whip from the desk.)* To the electric
hysteria of fear. *(She cracks the whip, making JOSEPH jump
back.)* Now confess.

JOSEPH: It wasn't my fault he died, I tell you. It was an
accident!

TAMARA: They say skin creates a devastating sky-cloth.
Especially if the skin is on a little boy's back. But if you
slash vermilion wounds on a boy's skin, they say you can
see such a sunset for miles. Which is why, rightly, you can
never forget all the exquisite pain. But then everything can
be measured except childhood pain. Yes...and I remember
once trimming my sister's fingernails with a whip like this.
But unfortunately she had an accident, and she lost her left
hand. Can't remember how. But then I once knew a sado-
masochist – not unlike you, Joe – though, of course, with
better manners. One Sunday evening, my machismo friend
cut open his left eyebrow with a scalpel that he'd taken

from a recently-deceased surgeon. Then he made a perfect incision…and so very, very slowly with, oh, such precision.

GRANDPA: You're doing awful things to my digestion. *(Belching loudly and clutching his abdomen.)* 'Fact it's getting noxiously noisy down here.

JANE: *(Ashen-faced.)* I'm not surprised.

JOSEPH: Look, how many times do I have to tell you, Fangers? It was an accident when my father broke his neck.

TAMARA: *(In her own world.)* And my friend's delicate but very deep cut in his own flesh was naturally in the shape of a capital Greek sigma. *(She uses her whip to illustrate the shape on her own face.)* The cut started here – on the bridge of his nose, and it threaded its way up through his eyebrow. As the cut descended, it curved around the top of his cheekbone until it touched the other side of his nose. Then the scalpel broke into a run as it gouged under his cheekbone, and the blade ended up by slicing off his ear with an artistic flourish that would have been a credit to Vincent Van Gogh. Not to mention Picasso's Rose period.

JOSEPH: I still have nothing to confess!

TAMARA: And his blood was so thrilled to get out – just like mine! Oh bloody hell! *(She pulls out a handkerchief and presses it to her nose.)* Thank Heavens, it's only a little squirt this time. Whereas my friend's blood bubbled down his chin before flowing along his jugular vein until his shirt looked like a matador's cape. So now he was utterly elated by the constant, ecstatic pain…

JANE: *(Now totally disconcerted.)* Look, you never told me you had a sister, Tamara. Oh I know I'm fairly drunk, and it's only just penetrated…but your sister… How exactly did she lose her hand?

TAMARA: Then as the blood fountained out of him and the pain continued to mount, my friend was in glorious Heaven. Depending, of course, on how you define Heaven.

And all the time my friend was gazing at his blood-soaked
self in his bed-sitter mirror. Like you, Joseph, he was a
total Narcissist. Well, all your shadow-fencing. What *is* it
covering up?

JOSEPH: You'd be terrified to know.

TAMARA: As for my friend, he started to slip and slide in
his own cascading blood. Then being a necromantic
practitioner in the Black Arts, he turned on the radio to
the Third Programme, and he began to rock-and-roll to
Tchaikovsky's *1812* overture. Yes, and simultaneously he
sang the ritual song of the Zulu virgins – oh for the Zulu
virgins! So there he was – can't you picture it, Joseph? –
doing what you'll be doing very soon – rocking-and-rolling
to an African fertility rite in his blood-spattered Bayswater
bedsit.

GRANDPA: Re-volting! Def-initely re-volting! I don't want to
hear anymore. God help my chop suey. I think it's about to
go straight through me. So what happened next. Don't tell
me!

TAMARA: He died – naturally, of course. Poor old Daddy. But
then no one understood you – save *me*. Did they, Daddy?

JANE: You mean, that totally obscene story, Tamara, is
about… your father?

TAMARA: Yes, but then the blood's always been in the flood in
our family. Just like Ganges.

JANE: But you told me you've never had a father. You've
always said that you were the result of the only messy
virgin birth in the history of the world. That's why
you claimed that you were born to be the Saviour of
Womankind.

JOSEPH: Yes, you're nothing but a pathetic failure, aren't you,
Fangers? And without the judo and the whip, you'd be just
a cowardy-custard wind-bag. What's more, I bet you've
never had a man. Not really frigging *had* one!

TAMARA: You were barely sixteen when you found your father
dead.

JANE: Why the constant lies, Tamara? You're often cruel, yes,
and disgusting, yes. I've come to expect all that. But not
these interminable lies.

TAMARA: And your father, Joseph, was found sprawled at the
bottom of your dung-coloured stairs, clutching a whip in
his hand. So your next-door neighbours laid your Daddy
out on the front-room table which strangely enough
was in the front room. Then the Police asked you about
the whip. You told them that your father had a yen for
foxhunting. By which time, Death had wrenched his face
into a gargoyle – very much like the one in your miniature
cathedral.

JOSEPH: You wouldn't know what to do with a man. Without
all the rubber and the contraptions.

TAMARA: Then you informed the Police that Daddykins
must've 'accidentally' tripped over your satchel, which
happened to be sitting conveniently at the top of the stairs,
packed with the Latin verbs for the dead. But, the truth
is, when your father discovered that you'd smashed all
the glasses, he screamed after you with his whip. *(flexing
the whip.)* And it was this very one, wasn't it? Then he
frenziedly flayed open your back until it resembled a
sunset. But despite the fact that you were fainting with
pain, you still managed to run up stairs. Then you threw
the satchel at his feet, and Daddy tripped over it. Then he
bounced down the stairs and slammed into the front door,
with a broken neck.

JOSEPH: Yes, and, rightly, the Judge's verdict was still
accidental death.

TAMARA: Your guts were revolted as you had to kiss his dead
open mouth with your dying lips.

JOSEPH: *(Now swigging vodka from the bottle.)* Look, stop
hiding behind my fabricated past. What about the endless

obscenities *you've* performed with my wife? *(Putting his arm around JANE's shoulders.)* Yes, and that's the real reason you're here, isn't it? Because you can't bear that I am possessing – and I'm going to possess 'your' Jane forever! That makes your Saphic gullet heave, doesn't it, Fangers? Continually thinking about *me* having what you once pawed over as yours. For the last six months you've thought of nothing else, save the electricity of her stockings shivering against my groin. Where were her hands marauding, you wondered? Where were my legs and phallus? 'Cause we certainly weren't seeking out your sunken Atlantis, that's for sure.

TAMARA: Yes, but I've never denied my sexual orientation. Never hidden behind family lies. And *I* didn't kill my father.

GRANDPA: I can't be doing with all this rapacious fighting. I'm so bloody hungry that me belly's a burping factory. Here comes another one. Hold on. *(Burping loudly.)* Oh that's a real aristocrat.

JANE: Go to bed, Dad, go to bed.

TAMARA: Yes, I find you utterly revolting, Grandpussy. Unfortunately for you.

GRANDPA: Joseph, I never told 'em what I found in the lettuce. And I never will. OOOH…here comes another. *(But his attempted belch turns into a cough.)* That burp went the wrong way, so now, for God's sake, just gimme something to nosh, Joseph.

TAMARA: You didn't divorce your wife, though, did you, Joe-schmo.

GRANDPA: I've never told Fanghorn nothing, Joseph, honest Injun. No one will ever know our secret, 'cause it's the only secret I've ever had. But I'm so totally famished that I can't rely on how long I'll keep it!

JOSEPH: You're talking too much again, Gramps. You know it
grates.

GRANDPA: Grates? Yeah, just gimme some grated cheese!

JANE: There's some cheese in the larder.

GRANDPA: No, there ent. I've just eaten it. And I've whipped
the last bits out of the mousetraps and noshed them, too.
And they were growing penicillin. But with a gut like mine,
you can't be choosy.

(TAMARA gives GRANDPA a fierce push.)

TAMARA: Shut-the-frig-up, you burnt-out faggot!

*(GRANDPA collapses on the carpet. JANE goes to him and helps him
into a chair.)*

JANE: I'll take you up to bed, Dad. Then, Tamara'll get what's
coming to her. 'Cause, believe me, with seagulls pecking
at you and half the beach in your fanny, well, that can be
most unpleasant. *(Now trying to prise GRANDPA out of his
chair.)* So let's ascend the wooden hill, Pops.

GRANDPA: *(Shaking JANE off.)* I'm all right, luv. *(Waving a
finger at TAMARA.)* You're about to regret what you did,
Fanghorn, 'cause now my wife will come and haunt you.
And let me tell you, that's some'at you won't forget.

TAMARA: Really? How nice for her.

JOSEPH: Plus you don't know what the lettuces are feeding on,
Fangers.

JANE: And once the sea embraces her, there's nowhere she
can hide from the seagulls' beaks.

GRANDPA: And my Missus will haunt you in the morning, and
when you're on the loo, too. She's no sense of decency. All
those years of decomposition takes it out of you something
rotten. 'Fact she's a complete walking anarchy. And, what's
more, she doesn't give a spectral toss! *(He staggers to the*

curtains.) And I've had it up to here with all them Satanic symbols!

(He pulls down the black drapes and the moonlight streams through the window.)

JANE: Right, Dad, now leave it be! Get off to bed. She's going to pay right enough. Aren't you, Tamara?

GRANDPA: No, no, this is my bit. The natural bit. It won't be as upmarket as the rest. I mean, there won't be a preponderance of blood, sex and violence and all that exciting with-it stuff. *(He wrenches open the French windows.)* 'Cause now the sea wants to come in. Yes, since the beginning of moving, of things moving, the sea has always wanted to come in, to swallow most of the things on Earth. And, Fanghorn, it's your kind of thing it wants most. Your girlish evil is its favourite food. Food? Food!! That reminds me; is there any Cornflakes left, Rice Crispies? Crisp ices? Fishy Pisces? Swish spices? Baby lices? Or anything nices?

TAMARA: You're completely senile, so you'll have to be terminated.

JOSEPH: I wonder whether the Prime Minister realises that all our debates on education, health welfare, pensions and national security, well, they all count for nothing, Fangers, in the face of something as negatively-predatory as you.

TAMARA: But you don't *know* the Prime Minister, Joe-Schmo. And you've never known him. Or spoken to him. Or to any other Minister, for that matter.

JOSEPH: *(Highly amused.)* Really?

TAMARA: Yes, 'really'.

JANE: But how can you say he doesn't know them, Tamara? Joseph's the First Secretary to the Minister of Defence!

TAMARA: Well, if he is First Secretary, then *I* am the *Minister* of Defence. *(JANE shakes her head in perplexed disbelief.)* Well, have you ever seen your husband's name on any State document? I mean, do you have any tangible proof that he is what he says he is?

JANE: Yes, he's shown me various letters from various Ministers. *(Suddenly unsure.)* At least he said they were from various Ministers. They were…printed, anyway. But I'm not interested in politics, so I've only taken a cursory glance at anything that he's shown me. Though, it's true, we've never been to any official dinner parties. And, for that matter, we haven't given any. But he insists work is work and home is home.

JOSEPH: Tamara, you do realise how dangerous this is all becoming, don't you? For all concerned. Chaucer's *Smyler with the Knyfe.*

TAMARA: Have you ever seen any photographs of your husband, Janey, in the newspapers? *The Times, Telegraph, Guardian, Evening Standard?* Or even, Karl-Marx-Help- Us, *The Daily Worker?*

JANE: No, but….

TAMARA: Oh, surely in your teaching job and social life, friends have asked you about your husband – as he has such an important position as First Secretary? Well, aren't they surprised that they don't recognise his name?

JANE: I never talk about him. He's mine. And everything he discusses with me is private. You see, he's told me that what he does involves State secrets, so everything that he shares with me should stay within these four walls. And it has. Well, that's the truth, isn't it, Joseph? *(JOSEPH remains silent.)* Joseph, support me, for God's sake! You deeply disturb me when you retreat into a… well, a glowering silence.

JOSEPH: The question is; who are you going to believe? Her or me? Who, Janey?

JANE: But you *are* the First Secretary to the Minister of
Defence, aren't you? *(JOSEPH continues to gaze at her.)* Look,
I never bothered to question whether you...

TAMARA: *(Overriding her.)* Never questioning and the
acceptance of appearances are culpable faults. Often
cancer only reveals itself when it is absolutely irrevocable.

JOSEPH: So *who* do you believe, Janey?

JANE: For Christ sake, Joseph, show her that letter of
commendation you received from the P.M. *(Opening
his desk drawer.)* It's in here, isn't it? *(Shuffling through the
papers.)* I'm sure I saw it the other day... *(Trailing off.)* Yes,
and why ever didn't I let you show me that photograph
album of you in China, when you went on that Peace
Mission for the Government? You know the mission that
you'd completed just after your divorce came through. You
are divorced, aren't you? Of course you are! You've got
the papers to prove it. You must have! I mean, for a start,
that vicar friend of yours has to have seen them. Well, you
must have shown them to him, or he would never have
married us. Mind, he went off to South Africa soon after,
and he *did* marry us in his church at...midnight. I've never
understood the midnight bit. And during the ceremony, he
did say that most vicars preferred not to marry divorcees –
I'm not a divorcee, of course – but that he said he'd agreed
to make an exception in our case. Yes, but why did we get
married at midnight, Joseph?

JOSEPH: A moonlight wedding is ultra romantic.

GRANDPA: Yes, it's getting crazier by the second. But then, I
suppose, when Fanghorn jumped into bed with me under
the table, I knew that the hunt was on. But I still want to
bloody know who is bloody hunting bloody who?

TAMARA: Shut up, you ancient crone, or I'll dispatch you into
the backend of next week.

JOSEPH: Don't you dare raise your infernal hand against my
confidant. The First Secretary to the Minister of Defence

does not advise it! *(As if he is dictating.)* And you may take that down, Miss Cuddles. *(Now in an imaginary Cabinet meeting.)* Yes, and unfortunately, Prime Minister, that is something that the Chinese will never understand. With their trillions of Communist disciplined, mass labourers, they still can never compete with a solitary Englishman's sacred amateur status. Because even death is amusing to an upstanding, clean-living Englishman. At least I've always regarded death as a bit of a giggle. In my more advanced experiments, that is.

TAMARA: Yes, and some believe that murder has also got great comic potential.

JANE: Where did you say your photograph album and your divorce papers were?

JOSEPH: I didn't.

JANE: Look, none of this is amusing anymore. So tell me where are they, Joseph?

JOSEPH: In my bureau in my bedroom. Or *our* bedroom. If you prefer it. That's, of course, if there's any time left for preferences.

JANE: Right. I'll show you, Tammers. Because he may have lied about his family background, but I know he's telling the truth about his job. And his divorce! At least I'm sure of that.

(She exits upstairs. GRANDPA, who has fallen asleep in the interim, emits a snore.)

TAMARA: Oh look, Grandpussy has nodded off. Mind, but for the swinish snuffles, you'd never know he was alive, would you. *(She offers JOSEPH a cigarette.)* Why don't we singe the old bastard's eyebrows? We'd both enjoy that. But unfortunately the smell would probably wake him up.

JOSEPH: *(Taking a cigarette.)* I never smoke. Makes me sick.

TAMARA: If fags didn't make you sick, there'd be little point in offering you one. Especially as your father forced you to eat a tobacco-sandwich when you were a boy.

JOSEPH: The interminable hours you must have put into studying my history.

(He crumbles the cigarette between his fingers.)

TAMARA: And the moment you'd eaten the tobacco-sandwich, you were promptly sick all over your Dad's smoking jacket.

JOSEPH: Yes…off the record, exactly how long have you been a sexy-clothes member of the Metropolitan Police Force?

TAMARA: And concerning the nature of the fertilisers in your lettuce-patch – could you elucidate?

GRANDPA: *(Waking up.)* Lettuce? Where's the lovely lettuce? I'm so hungry, I could eat it unwashed, maggots and all!

JOSEPH: (*To TAMARA.*) Everything's beginning to fit. You've only seen my wife at very selected intervals for the last year and a half because you've been working for the CID. On unsolved 'accidents'. Yes, let's call them that.

TAMARA: So where is your recent wife? Recently?

JOSEPH: D'you think Janey's having trouble finding my Chinese scrapbook and divorce papers?

GRANDPA: Look, would one of you kindly answer the other's question without asking another question before the previous unanswered question's answered? My ghostly wife does things like that. It's enough to give you piles.

(JANE re-appears empty-handed.)

JANE: I can't find the album, the divorce papers, or anything about you. There's nothing there. Who or…what the hell are you, Joseph? You're beginning to seriously frighten me.

TAMARA: *(Extending her hand to JANE.)* Man is evil, darling. Remember?

(JANE doesn't move.)

JANE: I deserve an explanation, Joseph.

JOSEPH: Explanation?

JANE: Yes, an explanation!

JOSEPH: And *pommes de terre.*

JANE: Look, I married you in good faith, Joseph. I'm not a complicated person but often I find it difficult to explain myself. Not because my silence is profound. It's not. But because everyone else explains their own private frills and flounces so much better than I do. So, on the whole, I prefer to say nothing, and ask nothing. But I have loved you, Joseph, as much as I'm capable. And I've always performed in bed.

JOSEPH: Adroitly.

JANE: And I've given you cough stuff when you've had a cough. Galloways. Plus I've kept the smell of oil-paints out of the house, because I know you don't like it. So I've done all my painting in that rotten shed. And give or take, I've been pretty faithful. *(TAMARA laughs.)* Well, I have done my best for what it's worth. But now it turns out that you may not be the first Secretary to the Minister of Defence, and you may have murdered your father. And what you've done to Mary, your last wife, God only knows!

JOSEPH: Experiments turn, Janey. Suddenly the tormented man seizes the flask of bubbling sulphuric acid, and he hurls the acid back into his tormentors' faces. Then he glories as their boiling flesh erupts all over his carpet.

JANE: What are you saying?!

JOSEPH: I'm saying that…I'll fetch Jackie. She may be able to explain the principles of fertilisation. *(He laughs.)* And the burial of the dying.

(He exits upstairs.)

JANE: *(To GRANDAD.)* Dad, you know something you're not telling. So tell us!

GRANDPA: Oh, look, here's Wolfy. *(Stroking Wolfy.)* Where've you been, you naughty doggy-pussy? Come to Mummy. Oooh… you've got dirty paws. Have you been digging up the garden again? Yes, you have, you wicked canine feline. You've got vine leaves weaved in your hair. So long live Henrik Ibsen is what I say.

JANE: Dad, for mercy's sake, you've got to tell me the truth. Is my husband a…? Well, is he a murderer?

GRANDPA: It's all different now, ent it, Wolfy? 'Cause she wants something from me now. Before it was 'You're too old, Dad, you're senile, you're lousy, smelly and hungry.' And I bloody am! If it goes on like this inside me guttage, I'll have to eat Wolfy. And I was very ill after I had my last doggy-pussy steak. But then I know only too well where a pussy-dog's been.

TAMARA: I'm going to burn off your eyebrows, Grandpa.

GRANDPA: I've got no eyebrows. I was so bloody hungry, I ate them this morning.

(JACKIE appears in the stair doorway, hugging HUMPH. JOSEPH has his arm around her. They are both laughing.)

JACKIE: Oh you are a one, Daddy. Well, it was such an outrageous thing to say with Humphy listening.

(JACKIE yawns.)

TAMARA: So what happened to your real mother, Jackie?

JACKIE: What's it got to do with you? And I'm not going to London. 'Cause Daddy says you're just a dirty, young

dyke. You don't look like a water-way to me, but he says
you're polluted.

TAMARA: Still not ready to confess, then, Joseph? So I shall
have to tell your wife and daughter what you really do
during the day, when you're supposed to be in the House
of Commons.

JOSEPH: There's no going back once you open the doors to
the Halls of Bedlam.

JACKIE: Have you been telling more porky-pies, then, Daddy?
So you're not the First Secretary to what-not, then. But
when I helped you put Mummy away, you promised
you'd be a good boy, and that you wouldn't tell any more
porkies. 'Specially as it was horrible what we did.

JOSEPH: Shut up. You're drunk.

JACKIE: You're proud of your lying, aren't you? Well,
someone's got to tell the truth. We've kept it quiet long
enough.

JOSEPH: If you do, dear, they'll lock me up as a maniac. And
you wouldn't like that – because for the rest of my life, I'll
be on bread and water.

GRANDPA: Where? Where's the bread? I'll give anything for a
nibble.

JOSEPH: *(To TAMARA.)* Alright, here it comes. It was two years
ago and thirteen days. Mary's birthday in fact. I'd tried all
the subtle ways to quiet her. Ground toadstools and deadly
nightshade, injecting nitric acid and things…

JACKIE: You are joking. You must be!

JOSEPH: I couldn't strangle her. I tried. With her stocking. But
her neck was like a tree trunk. Oak tree. 'Fact two oak tree
trunks. Her stocking snapped. It was a bit embarrassing
at the time. I think she took it personally. Women do,
you know. I even tried knocking a six-inch nail into her
forehead. The nail bent. So I straightened it out and had

another go. The hammer broke. And my old Dad – who was dead at the time – said to me; 'Pump icing sugar into her veins.' She used to like icing sugar. Well, as you know, my father was very artistic. Made marvellous doughnuts, with 'whipped' cream.

TAMARA: That's when he wasn't whipping you.

JOSEPH: Naturally. So on the evening of my first wife's birthday, after she'd gorged herself silly on eight puce jellies, two icky chocky cakes…

GRANDPA: *(Interrupting.)* Cakes? Help! I give in. Tell me where the puce icky-chockys are, and I'll take you to my leader.

JOSEPH: Plus six bottles of barley-water, nine doughnuts, fifteen four-pence-ha'penny meringues, three whippy ice-creams with lots of chocky on 'em, half her birthday cake and eight hamburgers with crackle pop onions.

GRANDPA: *(Salivating and crying.)* Oh for just one crackle-pop onion, I'll tell you where her body is!

JOSEPH: Don't rush, Grandpa, she's in no hurry. Well, there my wife was bloated on the bed, looking remarkably like a Christmas pudding – which looks very remarkable with breasts. So I stood and watched a tyre of rubber-blubber edge its way to where she used to keep her waist. Then I broke into a sweat. Well, it really was quite a sight. Because I knew from the expression of her hips that any minute now she was about to give birth to lemon meringues. And I have a particular aversion to lemon meringues produced in this original manner. So I gently inserted my home-made syringe full of home-made icing-sugar right up her… main artery. Then I pumped in the lot. It was lovely. She sweetened into death.

GRANDPA: If I'd've been there, I'd've had a couple of very large slices off her. Plus all them lemon meringues.

JACKIE: Then Daddy and I cut her up on the kitchen table which happened to be in the kitchen. With the birthday-cake knife. It was slow going. Big gorgey slices of her. She didn't bleed much. Only the occasional drop of raspberry yoghurt and clotted cream. Ooooh…it was so lovely licking her off my fingers.

TAMARA: Thank you very much, Jackie, and good night! *(She holds out a box of chocolates to GRANDPA.)* These chockys are all for you, Grandpussy. So now tell us where her body is.

(GRANDPA stuffs the chocolates into his mouth without taking the wrappers off.)

GRANDPA: Wonderful, wonderful. But I prefer 'em skinned. *(Spitting the wrappers out.)* She's under what's left of the lettuces. They're noshing her at this very moment. Sorry, Joseph, but I was so famished, I couldn't keep our secret any longer.

TAMARA: Right, now move your arse, Grandpa. Together we're going to do a spot of excavation in the garden. And you will hang for this, Joseph.

(Smiling JOSEPH produces a torch out of his desk drawer and he hands it to TAMARA.)

JOSEPH: Try not to break your necks in the dark. There are trip-wires and booby-traps everywhere – for the rabbits, now myxomatosis is out of season.

GRANDPA: *(Clicking his fingers.)* Come on, Wolfy. Mummy's got one lovely chocky left for you. But you've got to dig her up, boy, dig her up. Then I promise I'll keep me thieving hands off your kitty-litter.

(TAMARA, GRANDPA and WOLFY exit into the garden. JOSEPH sits on the table.)

JOSEPH: Jackie, come and sit by your Daddy with Humphy. See, this is the intermission. *(JACKIE sits on his right.)* So are you enjoying the movie, Janey? With the Father, the Daughter and the rolly-polly Ghost.

JANE: You can't really be so repellent. Why haven't I seen any
of this before?

JOSEPH: Actions should be taken for what they are, Janey.
Where there is laughter, you should hear only laughter. But
Tamara's got Freud on the groin and the brain. She's the
one who'll say that you're only laughing 'cause underneath
you're really lusting to get into your Great Aunt Clara's
pants, and that your Great Aunt Clara is, in fact, the Sex
Goddess Lilith, who is forever coupling with an Egyptian
scarab, which, as you know, is a dung-beetle. So once
you start questioning everything, then there is no end to
anything. You've got to accept things as they are. Well,
have *I* ever asked whether your teaching or your painting
are a cover for something else? Or because of what
you've done, whether one day you will be ready to have
children? Or have I demanded to know what your sexual
experiences were before you met me? No. Only when
the blood-sucker catalyst arrived did all these destructive
questions start. It was Fanghorn who brought all this
violence, filth and humiliation into our house. And now
we're left only with suspicion and an ever-growing fear.

JANE: But you still haven't answered anything, Joseph? Are
you divorced? Are you First Secretary? And, far more
important, did you murder your father and your wife?

JOSEPH: You've become the Unholy Inquisition, Janey, so the
verdict is yours. But one thing's certain; if I am lying about
being a senior civil servant, then my whole life is a make-
believe. And if I have murdered my father and my wife,
then I'll surely kill Tamara, and Grandpa – and may be
even you; because fatal experiments must continue until all
is resolved.

*(GRANDPA and TAMARA re-enter from the garden. GRANDPA holds a
spade and TAMARA a garden fork. GRANDPA has a green leaf hanging
out of his mouth, which he gobbles down as he enters.)*

GRANDPA: God, what was left of them lettuces was really
delish!

TAMARA: But there's nothing in the lettuce-patch. Only lettuce! And Grandpa's eaten them. So where is her body, Joseph?

JOSEPH: In the torturing laboratories of your mind, Fanghorn. The murders only exist in your heart. Like twin cancers, they're feeding off your soul. You see, one day, when you weren't looking, Evil climbed into the labyrinth of your brain, and it has been manipulating you ever since.

TAMARA: I'm not beaten yet. I intend to *have* you!

(JOSEPH grabs TAMARA, and before she can stop him, he kisses her voraciously full on the mouth. Then he rubs his body against her.)

JOSEPH: So would you like to 'have' me here on your Satanic altar? Or upstairs in the bath? With only Humphy watching our humping.

(TAMARA backs away from him in disgust, hastily covering her nose with a handkerchief.)

TAMARA: The blood's trying to get out 'cause the kiss disgusted it! This time it could be torrential. I think I need a doctor. Help me, Grandpa.

GRANDPA: No, I'm staying here. *(Stuffing the remaining wrapped chocolates into his mouth.)* Where the grub is!

JOSEPH: Oh no, you're not. You're just a gutsing stranger who couldn't keep a secret. So you'd better get out of here before you start decomposing like the body – which could turn up under our noses any time now.

TAMARA: *(With her handkerchief pressed against her nose.)* Heaven help me, it's like Noah's Flood!

GRANDPA: But I can't go with her. She isn't human, that one.

JOSEPH: *(Smiling.)* No, she's a bleeding woman. Like *you'll* be, Gramps, if you don't skidaddle with her pronto.

TAMARA: There's no way I'll ever leave you, Joseph. What's more, I'll have your whole garden dug up in the morning, and all the wallpaper torn off all the walls to find what's behind the plaster. Then I'll have all the plumbing ripped out until I discover what you're hiding, and where. And I will personally search your attic and cellar.

JOSEPH: With a warrant, you will – which you haven't got.

TAMARA: Oooh all my blood is so happy to get out, God help me!

JOSEPH: There's no way He's going to do that.

(TAMARA runs upstairs.)

GRANDPA: *(Pitifully.)* Tell me another secret, Joseph, and I'll keep this one.

JOSEPH: Into the sea with you, you burbling intestine.

GRANDPA: *(Tearfully.)* How can you just sit there, our Janey, with yer head in yer hands? Come away with me now! 'Cause one thing's certain, Joseph; my wife will haunt the beJesus out of you.

JANE: That's the least he deserves, Dad.

GRANDPA: Then, Janey, will you come…?

JANE: *(Overriding him and seizing her father's hand.)* Yes, and I'm coming with you this instant. *(To JOSEPH.)* I'll send someone round for all our clothes and things because there's nothing for us here. Only frightening questions. No, really, Joseph. What, in life's name, *are* you?

(Hand in hand JANE and GRANDPA exit through the Stage Left door which leads them out of the house. They are never coming back. JACKIE watches them go. Laughing she rushes into her father's arms.)

JACKIE: They've gone, Daddy. Just like you said they would. Yes, it's been a right giggle, hasn't it, Humphy? And didn't I do my role well, Dadsy? All that rubbish about cutting up Mumsy on the kitchen table that happened to be in the kitchen.

JOSEPH: You'll make a marvellous actress one day, my love.

JACKIE: Won't I just? I especially liked the bit where we got angry with each other. The idea of you being a multiple murderer. Ridiculous. And everyone knows that you're the First Secretary to the Minister of…whatever you're the First Secretary to the Minister of, don't they? *(Moving to the stair doorway with Humph in her arms.)* Now close the window, Daddy. The sea's still trying to get in. Then come up and tuck me up.

JOSEPH: *(Closing the window.)* I will, but leave Humph with me. I always like to have a good-night chat with him. Even though he does stink.

(JACKIE thrusts Humph into JOSEPH's arms, then she goes up to bed.)

JACKIE: *(Off.)* But don't forget to come and tuck me in!

JOSEPH: *(Calling after her.)* I won't, darling. But it was marvellous truth-telling tonight. *(He sits Humph next to his cathedral.)* So, Humphy-dumfy, how will we make Janey disappear? With sand in her navel? And what about Grandpops? Under what's left of the lettuce patch? They'll never look there twice. And, most important of all, what about our favourite dyke, Fecund Fanghorn? Shall I cut a Greek sigma into her eyebrow with my scalpel? *(He picks up the telephone and dials.)* Yes, well, I'm sorry to wake you, Prime Minister, but I'm about to have a prolonged holiday. So, for once, you'll have to sort out Emperor Mao and his coolies on your own. But then I understand the Chinese love picking English brains. Especially if they're pickled – as an hors d'oeuvres. *(He hangs up the phone, and opens the French doors.)* And after a death or three, to the time of the sea, I think I'll go on another Peace Mission with my scrapbook somewhere out there… *(Looking at the sea.)* Yes, now it's all working out lusciously. Ecstasy is what it's about, and chopped diamonds and pelicans' tonsils…

(TAMARA appears in the doorway in a very revealing negligee.)

TAMARA: …With garlic and chop suey. And now we'll to bed, where we will get on with it. 'Cause my nose-bleed's over, and we've years and years at our disposal. *(Slowly she undulates towards him.)* But first…confess.

JOSEPH: I've nothing to confess. *(When they are a yard apart, JOSEPH pulls out a gun and fires it point-blank at her face. The squirting liquid from the gun streams down her negligee. She covers her face and screams as he pockets his pistol. He laughs.)* Yes, unfortunately it's not nitric acid. But one day soon you'll wish it was. *(He giggles violently.)* Oh it's going to be marvellous. You'll adore it; the exquisite endless pain that's in store. Until death us do part, my lovely.

(TAMARA smiles as she moves closer to him.)

TAMARA: Oh much, much longer than that…

(TAMARA FANGHORN's smile broadens as she opens her mouth fully to reveal – for the first time – that she has the fangs of a vampire!

As if hypnotised, JOSEPH exposes his neck, and FANGHORN prepares to bite him as…the CURTAIN falls.)

THE END

EDRED, THE VAMPYRE

Characters

EDRED

ELIZABETH

JACQUES

By the altar of Saint Lawrence's Church, in the village of Cholesbury. Hertfordshire.

Time; the Present. Dusk. Early autumn.

The church is empty save for the rapidly-gathering evening shadows. In the distance there is a growl of thunder.

Off stage, a key is heard turning in a protesting lock. Then there is the creaking sound of the outer church door being pushed open. This is followed by an echoing clang as the church door is closed.

A moment later the hooded figure of EDRED appears, swathed in a black cloak. As he enters, he thrusts something into his trouser pocket. Then EDRED pushes back his hood, and looks around the church. EDRED is weary, but he is still seductively dangerous. Then he sits on the altar rail and stares sightlessly into space.

Another thunder growl. EDRED continues to gaze into the void.

There is the sound of a tentative but echoing rap on the church's outer door. EDRED rubs his eyes.

Silence, followed by a second knock on the church door. EDRED smiles.

Silence, followed by a third knock on the outer door.

EDRED: Why do you keep on knocking when you know you can come straight in? Yes, I was fully aware you were watching me while I was unlocking the church door. *(There is the creaking sound of the church door being opened tentatively.)* That's the ticket. *(Silence.)* It's too late now to hesitate on the threshold. Instead – as Shakespeare would have said, had he thought of it; 'Stay not upon your coming, but come.' *(Silence, followed by another rumble of thunder.)* You know you want to, and need to. Otherwise you wouldn't have followed me here so diligently. *(Smiling.)* Yes, yes, I do appreciate the fear you're feeling. It's almost tangible, isn't it? And so delectable. Like anticipating the night's first exquisite taste of blood. Which you have to savour thoroughly before you…swallow it. *(More thunder but nearer.)* Look, there's no point in you shivering and just

dithering in the doorway because I can hear your hectic
breathing even from here. So 'screw your courage to the
sticking-place, and you'll not fail.' Yes, and old Sweet
Willy Shakebag *did* say that. *(Silence. A shimmer of lightning,
followed by a crack of thunder.)*
Or if you are so totally overwhelmed with dread,
Close the church door, and run home through the Dead,
And live with your fearful dreams in your desolate trundle
bed.
Yes, I know, I know; the timing
And chiming
Of rhyming.
But the rhymer's craft becomes second nature when you
have lived as long as I have, and frequented all those
other sleepless worlds. *(Silence, followed by more thunder.)*
Now this is becoming pointless. You're obviously so…
Overwhelmed with angst, foreboding and woe,
You should just close the church door now, and go.
Then what you came here for, you will never know;
But the haunting of the Living Dead will go on and on,
And there will be no end to your tortured, sleepless song.

*(Long pause, followed by the sound of the church's outer-door
clanging shut.*

*There is an ear-splitting crash of thunder as ELIZABETH, a comely
18-year-old, enters. She is followed by JACQUES, who is equally
good-looking, and who is also 18. They are both carrying large,
bulky camping rucksacks.*

*ELIZABETH stops some distance from EDRED. Then she stares at the
motionless EDRED, who remains seated on the altar rail. ELIZABETH
is obviously disconcerted by this, but EDRED still doesn't move. He
just smiles at her.*

*Now uncertain what to do, ELIZABETH turns to JACQUES, who
shakes his head disparagingly.)*

JACQUES: This is a total waste of time.

(ELIZABETH turns back to EDRED, who continues to smile at her.)

ELIZABETH: Look, we're sorry but we've made a mistake.

EDRED: I'm not what you expected, right?

ELIZABETH: We didn't know what to expect. *(She indicates JACQUES.)* But he's right. There's no way *you're* a…a…well, like…a vam…pire, is there? *(There is a flash of lightning followed by a deafening crack of thunder.)* Well, you're not… are you?

EDRED: Straight to the point. I like that. *(With a toothy smile.)* Or would you prefer…'points'?

(JACQUES gestures at EDRED's mouth.)

JACQUES: *(Laughing.)* If you're a vampire – where's your fangs?

EDRED: *(Amused.)* They're retractable.

JACQUES: *(To ELIZABETH.)* Let's get outta here. This is a waste of time.

ELIZABETH: Hang on, hang on. If he's not a vampire, then… *(To EDRED.)* Then…well, why you wearing that black cloak?

EDRED: Old habits die young. But then; so do most *people.*

JACQUES: Very cute. *(To ELIZABETH, under his breath.)* Look, stop staring at him, and let's go.

EDRED: She's staring, and she's not going – because she knows. *(After another growl of thunder, EDRED smiles at ELIZABETH.)* Don't you?

ELIZABETH: So you're really like claiming you're a…well, a real…vampire, then?

EDRED: I don't have to claim; it's an on-going reality.

JACQUES: No way!

EDRED: *(To JACQUES.)* And behind all your Sixth-Form College bravura, *you* believe I am, too. *(EDRED gestures at the shimmering lightning.)* Or you wouldn't have braved the prospect of a nocturnal storm, and come to the church with her to find me, would you? *(Smiling.)* But more amusingly, how did you hear of me?

ELIZABETH: We… Well, it's hard to explain, but we…Googled you.

EDRED: *(Smiling.)* Yes, what would the world do without Google? And I fitted the description of The Hertfordshire Vampire, right?

JACQUES: Well…yeah. And there was quite a lot of stuff about you on Wikipedia, too.

EDRED: Hardly surprising as 'wiki' is the Hawaiian word for 'fast', and Wikipedia's so fast, it generally gets everything wrong. *(To ELIZABETH.)* But, more to the point, how did you find me?

ELIZABETH: Well, two days ago this guy…think his name was Rob Cowan…well, he posted on the Web that he saw you on Cholesbury Common in the moonlight, carrying something under your cloak. But when he tried to approach you, you ran 'cross the cricket pitch and disappeared into the trees, and then you were like… swallowed up in the mist.

EDRED: Mm…it seems for once the Web's got something vaguely right. *(EDRED mimes the execution of a square-cut.)* But then I've always had a penchant for cricket.

JACQUES: A vampire that likes cricket? Now you're really taking the piss.

EDRED: If that is all I 'take', then it will be least of your problems. But how did you so conveniently find me tonight?

ELIZABETH: We were sitting in the garden of 'The Half Moon', just before closing time, when I felt like…drawn to come here to…look for you…

EDRED: Just as I surmised.

JACQUES: But I knew to get here that we'd have to go through
St Laurence graveyard in the dark, so I told her it'd be best
to wait 'till morning.

ELIZABETH: And I said we had to go through the graveyard
tonight. Well, you wouldn't be here in the morning
'cause…well, come sunrise, I knew you'd have to…
y'know…like go back to your…well, y'know, your…
your…

(Another crack of thunder.)

EDRED: *(Amused.)* …Coffin?

ELIZABETH: Right!

EDRED: I don't have to do that.

JACQUES: You don't?

EDRED: No. Jumping into coffins at sunrise is optional.

ELIZABETH: So Wikipedia's…?

EDRED: *(Overriding her .)* Yes, that's just another of the
countless misconceptions about vampires you'll find
peppered all over the Internet. However, it's not
surprising… *(He points at ELIZABETH.)* …that *you* felt – as
you so appositely put it – 'drawn' to come here to find me.
Many before you have been 'drawn' by much the same
compulsion. And now, of course, your desire to uncover
the truth about me, combined with your fear, is proving to
be the most potent of aphrodisiacs, isn't it?

ELIZABETH: No!

EDRED: Especially as you are haunted.

ELIZABETH: I'm not haunted!

EDRED: It's lurking behind your eyes. And eyes never lie.

JACQUES: *(Under his breath to ELIZABETH.)* Look, he's messing
with you, 'cause he's just another mouthy fake.

EDRED: And *you*, of course, would know. Especially as you have both been searching for me for…what?…barely two weeks now in your summer break.

ELIZABETH: How'd you know that?

EDRED: That's only the tip of the iceberg of what I'm learning about you.

JACQUES: Go on then; tell us something else 'bout us that isn't just another lucky guess.

(EDRED points to ELIZABETH.)

EDRED: You've a hair on your sleeve. Give it to me.

ELIZABETH: Why?

JACQUES: Don't give it him!

EDRED: What harm can I do with a hair of her head?

JACQUES: Tons! Well, we've read enough about witchcraft to know what you can do with a human hair.

EDRED: Yes, and it was your extra-curricular studies into the Occult that was mainly responsible for *you* getting…an A Star in Biology and an A in History, and, but *only* a D in French; so *she's* going up to Cambridge, and you're not.

JACQUES: How'd you know all that?

EDRED: 'Cause I'm the antithesis of everything you've ever Googled, or gleaned from Wikipedia. But then I have been around almost forever, so I am rather long in the tooth. Or should I say…teeth?

(Still smiling EDRED stands. Then he moves towards ELIZABETH and JACQUES, who hastily retreat from him.)

ELIZABETH: Oh no!

(EDRED points to a pew.)

EDRED: Look, why don't you both take the weight off your feet? Your rucksacks look incredibly heavy, so you've obviously crammed them to the seams... *(With an approving smiling.)* ...with numerous parts of dismembered bodies.

JACQUES: No, we've not! We've not dismembered anything! Or *anyone!* That's more *your* style.

EDRED: Touché – as the French would say. Though, as you will discover, historically – like you, with your D in French – I, too, have developed an aversion to the Frogs. So if your rucksacks aren't bursting with dismembered parts...?

ELIZABETH: *(Overriding him.)* It's just our camping gear and...

EDRED: *(Completing her thought, with another smile.)* ...The odd weapon you plan to use against the Living Dead.

ELIZABETH: We've come prepared.

JACQUES: So don't try anything!

EDRED: I don't have to, now that I know that you've both been wasting so much of your time Googling vampiric nonsense.

(EDRED brushes past ELIZABETH and JACQUES. In their panic they run behind the altar.)

ELIZABETH: Where you going?

(EDRED exits.)

EDRED: *(Off.)* To ensure we're not disturbed.

JACQUES: *(To ELIZABETH.)* Told you this was a crazy idea!

ELIZABETH: Yes, but what's the point of us finding him if we don't...?

JACQUES: *(Overriding her.)* No, no; you're right. And there are two of us, and we're younger and much stronger than he is. *(JACQUES takes off his rucksack and taps it with his foot.)* And if he tries anything, 'least we're armed.

ELIZABETH: And we've got our mobiles! *(She takes off her rucksack.)* Anyway, he looks tired. And somehow...well, kind of like...vulnerable.

(EDRED returns.)

EDRED: You should never let appearances fool you. Especially as the night is young. But then the night is always young – for me.

JACQUES: Hm! You don't fool me. Well, you're all mouth and no trousers.

EDRED: *(Smiling.)* You can certainly rely on my mouth.

(In response ELIZABETH pulls her mobile out of the flap of her rucksack.)

ELIZABETH: Look, if you try to do anything to us, we'll call the Police.

EDRED: Be my guest.

ELIZABETH: I will call them!

EDRED: Then do so.

JACQUES: She means it.

EDRED: So do I. But she'll never get through. You see, I've always found that in most churches the reception is unusually bad. Probably because there are a multitude of angels clogging up the air-waves. *(JACQUES laughs.)* I'm glad you find it funny.

JACQUES: Not laughing at that. Laughing at *you*! 'Cause you're no more a vampire than I am. Well, for starters; vampires don't make jokes.

EDRED: Don't they? Then you obviously didn't Google Dr Scoffern's 'Stray Leaves of Science and Folklore' – because Scoffern correctly asserts that 'a vampire is a living, murderous and *mischievous* dead body.' But then the Doctor judiciously added; 'Of course my words are idle, contradictory and incomprehensible, but then, of course… *(Smiling.)* …so is a vampire.'

JACQUES: Right, we've heard enough of your phoney vampire crap. So gimme the key you've put in your pocket. I know you just locked the church door with it. Then we'll be on our way, and you can go on making your stupid jokes 'till you're blue in the face.

EDRED: Do you know how old I am?

JACQUES: You could be any age. Now gimme the key!

EDRED: *You* both believe you're going to live forever, don't you?

ELIZABETH: What?

EDRED: Secretly you do. In your heart of hearts. Well, when you're eighteen – and that's what both of you are – the idea that one day you will actually die seems utterly nonsensical, doesn't it? Death is still so very far away from you. Yet the reality is, death is always so much nearer than you think. Unless you're a vampire, of course. And then you can live – God help you -almost forever. *(EDRED goes behind the altar, and thrusts his hand under the hem of the altar cloth.)* And one of the reasons you're here is you would like to know *how* you can live forever. Well, I'm right, aren't I?

JACQUES: What are you…getting from behind there?

EDRED: A drink. It'll help us to get to know one another. *(With a flourish EDRED produces a bottle of wine and three goblets.)* Well, all I can say is… *(as he opens the bottle.)* … thank the Devil for screw tops!

ELIZABETH: That's not…Communion wine, is it?

EDRED: No, it's blood. Of the New Testament. *(He pours some wine into the three goblets on the altar.)* And this is, of course, why all Catholics are on their way to becoming vampires. *(EDRED smiles at ELIZABETH as he offers her a goblet.)* So I'm sure you would love a gulp of my crimson nectar, wouldn't you?

ELIZABETH: No!

EDRED: But you will, won't you, Jacques?

JACQUES: How'd you know my name?

EDRED: *(Smiling.)* I Googled you.

JACQUES: Very funny.

EDRED: Quite – because I don't need aids like the Internet to see the horrific images illuminating the screens… *(To both of them.)* …on the insides of your skulls.

JACQUES: And you still want us to believe you can do all that 'cause you're a vampire who's…well, like…lived almost forever?

EDRED: Yes, sadly that is the truth.

JACQUES: OK, OK; we can play games, too. Gimme the wine. 'Cause it *is* only wine, isn't it?

(EDRED puts the goblet back on the altar.)

EDRED: Take the goblet from the altar, and taste it. Then you'll discover what it is. If you have the guts, Jacques.

ELIZABETH: No, don't drink it, Jacques!

JACQUES: What've I got to lose? Well, I'm sure not even *he* goes in for bottling blood behind the altar.

(JACQUES picks up a goblet from the altar.)

ELIZABETH: No, no, you were right, Jacques! We should get outta here. And now! *(To EDRED.)* So gimme the key! *(EDRED smiles.)* Please!

(Still smiling EDRED produces the key from his pocket, and he places it on the palm of his other hand – which then he extends to ELIZABETH.)

EDRED: Here's the key. But you'll have to come and take it from me, Elizabeth.

ELIZABETH: How'd you know my name?

EDRED: Once you take the key from me, Elizabeth, things will grow infinitely clearer.

JACQUES: Don't take it!

(EDRED turns on JACQUES, and gives JACQUES a withering glare. In stunned response JACQUES, who is still holding his goblet, subsides into a pew as if he is spellbound.

Then EDRED turns back to ELIZABETH, with the key extended on the palm on his hand, and he whispers to her.)

EDRED: Elizabeth....

(As if in a trance, ELIZABETH nods. Then she crosses to EDRED, and reaches out to take the key. As ELIZABETH's fingers touch EDRED's palm, gently but firmly EDRED's fingers close around hers. Then slowly he pulls ELIZABETH towards him – while the now-seemingly-spellbound JACQUES watches in silence from the confines of his pew.

Then EDRED opens his mouth as he prepares to bite…ELIZABETH's neck, but she remains motionless as if she's been hypnotised by him. Then voluntarily she exposes her neck to EDRED, inviting EDRED to use her as he wishes. But after a long pause, EDRED draws back from ELIZABETH, leaving her neck untouched. Then he closes his mouth.

EDRED smiles at the still-entranced figure of JACQUES. Then luxuriantly he strokes ELIZABETH's neck with his other hand while he whispers in her ear.)

EDRED: All in good time, Elizabeth, all in good time. And then you will have everything you desire, and more – because you *are*…different. Yes…you most certainly are….

ELIZABETH: You're fingers are so…cold. But your skin, it's… well, it's like…on fire…

(JACQUES rubs his eyes fiercely, then he puts down his goblet and surges to his feet.)

JACQUES: Right, I've had enough of your vampire bilge. Now gimme the key!

EDRED: Certainly. But *you*, too, Jacques, will have to take the key from me.

ELIZABETH: *(To EDRED.)* No, don't you touch Jacques!

EDRED: *(Smiling knowingly.)* Why ever not, Elizabeth?

ELIZABETH: I just don't want you to.

JACQUES: I'm not scared of him! *(To EDRED.)* Now gimme the key.

ELIZABETH: That's not the reason I don't want you to touch him…

JACQUES: *(Overriding her.)* Look, stop messing about and gimme the bloody key!

EDRED: I know that's not the reason, Elizabeth. But as Jacques claims he's not frightened of me, he can take the 'bloody key' *from* me himself, can't he? *(EDRED smiles at JACQUES, who is now hovering uncertainly.)* Well, you can – can't you? *(Abruptly JACQUES lunges for the key, but EDRED is too quick for him, and he seizes JACQUES' wrist with his other hand. JACQUES struggles to free himself from EDRED's vice-like grip. Then suddenly all the energy seeps out of JACQUES. Helplessly JACQUES gazes in amazement at EDRED. In response EDRED smiles at him.)* So *now* what do *you* feel, Jacques? But then, of course, 'Jacques' is only your nom de plume, isn't it?

JACQUES: No, Mum really called me that 'cause she liked the sound of it.

EDRED: And you repaid her by almost failing French. But then, of course, your father has a different and far more apposite appellation for you, doesn't he? Because he knows the real you.

(As EDRED continues to grip his wrist, JACQUES whispers to EDRED in fearful disbelief.)

JACQUES: Who…in God's name…*are* you?

EDRED: *(Continuing to hold JACQUES' wrist.)* God has nothing do with me. But what *I* am…is over one-thousand-years-old. And, indeed, I am probably much, much older. Although, in truth, my first clear memory is of my brother,

Edmund, while he was celebrating St Augustine's Mass Day in Pucklechurch, when the exiled thief, Leofa, sprang up from behind the rood. Then Leofa butchered my brother in front of me. *(Dismissively EDRED releases JACQUES, who slumps back into his pew in a state of shock.)* That's why I have had so little time for churches ever since. Except, of course, they are moderately-pleasant places to have a quiet drink in, when you can't sleep. *(EDRED stares sightlessly into the middle distance.)* And I can never sleep. So it's pointless me closing my eyes. Yet wherever I look, I find I'm always staring into the eternal abyss of… myself.

(Still staring into the void, EDRED gestures towards the altar. In response ELIZABETH crosses to the altar, picks up a wine goblet. In a trance-like state, she drinks half of its contents. Then she rubs her eyes and refocuses. She turns back to EDRED.)

ELIZABETH: Yeah, but I still can't understand why… Well, why doesn't the Vicar ever *see* you come in here at night, and then have you, well…thrown out of his church?

EDRED: *(Amused.)* How can the Vicar throw me out? When he's hardly ever here. In fact the Vicar only comes to this church every other Sunday as he has rarely more than three villagers in his congregation. Because – unlike me – the Church of England is dying. So, on the odd occasions when the Vicar does turn up, I simply pop into the nearest available coffin. For the rest of the time, whenever I feel in need of a quiet night-cap… *(EDRED takes a goblet from the altar.)* …I use this as my private pub. And St Laurence Church was built in the middle of an Iron Age hillfort, so I'm hardly ever disturbed as very few unwanted folk dare to venture into these ancient purlieus after dark. *(EDRED smiles at JACQUES. In response, mechanically JACQUES picks up his goblet and drinks half of its contents.)* But, of course, there are still those – like you two – who feel undeterred because of the urgency of their mission. *(EDRED savours his drink.)* So fortunately there's never been a shortage of occult missionaries.

ELIZABETH: Yeah, but how'd you manage to get hold of the key to this church in the first place?

EDRED: I not only have a deft way with pecking passing necks, but I'm also rather deft at picking passing pockets. And once you've acquired someone's key, it's a breeze to have it copied. Which is why no one is ever completely safe.

JACQUES: But people must see there are lights on in here.

EDRED: What lights?

JACQUES: The candles.

(EDRED shakes his head and points at the candles.)

EDRED: They're not lit, are they? And I never light them. *(Amused.)* Don't need to.

ELIZABETH: Then how…?

EDRED: *(Finishing her thought.)* …Can *we see* each other, Elizabeth? Simple. The fire you both felt emanating from my flesh, *that* provides me with the Living Dead's equivalent to a corporeal halo. And although the light that radiates from me is softly seductive, and somewhat baleful… *(He watches them drink in unison.)* …it's still bright enough for you to see that you're drinking blood from those goblets, isn't it?

(JACQUES splutters into his goblet.)

JACQUES: Blood?!

ELIZABETH: 'S'not blood, Jacques! Well, it doesn't…taste like blood.

EDRED: When did *you* last taste blood, Elizabeth?

ELIZABETH: Yesterday. When I…accidentally bit my tongue.

EDRED: Yes, but when did you *really* last taste blood?

ELIZABETH: I just told you!

EDRED: You don't fool me. You see, when I touched you; I knew.

JACQUES: *(After tasting the wine again.)* No, she's right. It isn't blood. 'S'red wine. *(Reading the label on the wine bottle.)* 'Fact it's just a cool little… *(Pronouncing it incorrectly.)* …Reejoa.

EDRED: Spoken like a true blood-connoisseur. So, Elizabeth, would you like some more of this 'cool little… *(Pronouncing it correctly.)* …Rioja'?

JACQUES: You're trying to get her pissed, aren't you, you dirty git!

(EDRED advances on ELIZABETH with the wine bottle.)

EDRED: Don't heed him. You know your own mind. And your goblet's all but empty; so you need a soupcon more. Oh don't worry, we won't run out. I've another couple of bottles stashed away behind the altar. And, believe me, my wine is in quite a different league to the acrid plonk the Vicar serves up to his congregation of three – Erzebet.

ELIZABETH: I'm not 'Erzebet'!

EDRED: No. *(He smiles knowingly.)* Sorry…Elizabeth. For a moment, I forgot.

JACQUES: *(To ELIZABETH.)* What's he twatting on about now?

EDRED: All will come to fruition soon enough, Jacques. *(He continues to hold out the bottle to ELIZABETH.)* So now I'm sure you will have a vinous re-fill, won't you?

ELIZABETH: Well, it's not bad, so why not?

EDRED: Why not, indeed? *(He re-fills her goblet.)* 'In vino… veritas'. But first you need to know the truth about *me*, Elizabeth. And when you *hear* it, it's imperative you *believe* it. Only then will you begin to understand the truth about *yourself.* Because it was your desperate need to discover the truth about yourself that compelled you to come to me this evening.

ELIZABETH: That's not true!

EDRED: *(Refilling his own goblet.)* It is. What's more, it's your malefic dreams that have drawn you to me, Elizabeth. Your subconscious has told you that *I* have the key to resolving your nightmares. And tonight is as good a time as any to exorcise them. Or perhaps – even better – to fulfil them.

ELIZABETH: Look, I can kinda see how you can…well, sorta read our minds, and that's why you know things about us like…College and all that. But how can you know 'bout my nightmares?

JACQUES: He doesn't! He's just trying to freak you out.

ELIZABETH: No, Jacques, you're wrong! And *he* could be right – 'cause I've got to try and understand… *(She rubs her forehead fiercely.)* …what the hell's going on in *here*! And I feel…well, I feel perhaps he *can* help me. And I do need help.

JACQUES: You mustn't listen to him. He's just screwing with yer head!

ELIZABETH: Will you just shut up for once, Jacques! I've got to hear what he wants to tell me.

EDRED: And *you* must listen to me, too, Jacques. Because *you* have also been having horrendous nightmares, haven't you? Especially since you and Elizabeth have been sleeping together regularly.

JACQUES: I've not been having nightmares.

ELIZABETH: What's the point in lying, babes?

JACQUES: I'm not lying!

ELIZABETH: You are! Or why d'you keep waking me up during the night, and screaming at me in your sleep? Flailing your arms and laughing like a madman. And what you did the last two nights was even worse.

JACQUES: I did nothing the last two nights!

EDRED: Oh but you did, Jacques. And deep down, behind all your 'I-failed-to-get-into-Oxbridge-street-cred' bluster, you know the terrible things you did the last two nights. *(With a conjuror's flourish, EDRED produces another wine bottle from behind the altar and opens it.)* Because your dreams are now even worse than Elizabeth's. Which is why, equally, *you* felt compelled to come here to find me.

JACQUES: No, you're just guessing about my dreams. Well, how can you really know? You can't!

EDRED: *(Pouring wine into JACQUES' glass.)* Oh I can. And do. And the reasons will become only too apparent once I tell you what has happened to *me.*

JACQUES: *(Laughing in disbelief.)* You saying *I'm* going to turn into a vampire, too, then?

EDRED: No, but until you understand the horrific enormity of my life, you will never come to terms with the terrors that stalk your nightmares.

ELIZABETH: Then, for God's sake, tell us! How'd you... well, how'd you become like... well, like what you *say* you are now?

EDRED: *(Pouring her some wine.)* I told you that my first clear memory was of my brother being slain in Pucklechurch in front of me.

JACQUES: *(Laughing in disbelief.)* 'Slain'?

EDRED: Yes, Jacques, he was slain. But what I did *not* tell you was that my brother, Edmund, was also my sovereign liege-lord. So, as his two sons were scarcely more than infants when Edmund was killed in the year Nine Hundred and Forty-Seven, the Witan, which was the Royal Council, appointed *me*, his brother – instead of either of his underage sons – as the next Anglo Saxon King of England.

JACQUES: *(Laughing and spluttering into his goblet.)* You – the King of England?

EDRED: Yes, I was – and am King Edred. But then Edred is a very appropriate name for a vampire, don't you think? Especially as, nine centuries later, the great Sigmund Freud wrote that whenever anyone contemplates death, they always experience a morbid *dread.* So perhaps that's why my mother prophetically called me 'Ed-dred'.

JACQUES: Yeah, well, I've read all about *Ethelr*ed the *Un*ready, but…

EDRED: *(Overriding him.)* Well, *I* am *Ed*red the *Ever*-ready.

ELIZABETH: Yes, but even if you were – as you say – an Anglo Saxon king, still doesn't explain how you turned into… well, like into a vampire, does it?

EDRED: No. My vampiric transformation only came about because – as the new King of England – I had to repel the invading Norseman, Eric Bloodaxe, and his Northumbrian vassals.

JACQUES: Oh come off it, there's no way you could take on Bloodaxe and his vassals.

EDRED: I more than took them on. But the only way I could defeat them was by tragically consigning the town of Rippon and its Minster to the flames until all that was left was piles of smouldering flesh and rubble. And it was the searing memories of the horrendous devastation that *I* had caused that gave me endless sleepless nights. Indeed, it was the lack of sleep that brought about my fatal eating disorder.

JACQUES: *(Laughing.)* 'Fatal eating disorder'?

EDRED: Yes, even the Anglo Saxon Chronicles record the details of my eating disorder.

JACQUES: You're being serious, aren't you?

EDRED: Never more so – because, thenceforward, I couldn't digest any solid foods. I could only suck out the juices. Especially the blood out of chewed meat. Then I had to spit out everything else. So I was never able to eat enough to sustain me, and thus... *(With an ironic smile.)* ...I died when I was comparatively young.

ELZABETH: You...died?

EDRED: Yes. They buried me in the graveyard at Old Minster in Winchester, and that should have been the end of me.

JACQUES: Yeah, so why the Hell wasn't it?

EDRED: Hell...only knows. But, for several days, I lay dead in my coffin, and then...what I can only describe as...well, as some kind of energised...Satanic force possessed my dead body. Yes, suddenly I found I was imbued with the strength of ten men, so my now-seemingly-living corpse started to claw its way out of the grave. But as I hurled more and more of the soil from me, I discovered I had this insatiable thirst for...human blood. And through all the ages, my thirst has never been slaked. Although, it's true, I am now very weary of...everything. *(EDRED stares at them.)* Yet my lust for blood is undiminished.

ELIZABETH: That's rank!

EDRED: Indeed.

JACQUES: Oh get real, Lizzie. You don't really believe him, do you?

ELIZABETH: So where...did you go – Edred – after you became a... vampire?

EDRED: To the battlefields, where I could slake my demonic thirst. And there were always plenty of battlefields. Then once I was amongst the dead, I sucked their congealing blood from their butchered corpses.

ELIZABETH: Ugh! That's horrible!

EDRED: Yes, and there was no limit to the horror. Especially at the Battle of Sanguelac...

ELIZABETH: 'Sanguelac'?

JACQUES: *(Showing off his knowledge.)* Yeah, 'Sanguelac', babes, is what the Normans called their 'Lake of Blood' at the Battle of Hastings, when William defeated Harold Godwinson, and King Harold was killed with an arrow in his eye.

EDRED: *(Applauding him.)* Tres bon, Jacques, tres bon. No wonder you got an A Star in History. But what you don't know is…*I* was at the Battle of Sanguelac, too. And after the battle, I found King Harold's body, and then, knowingly, I drank his royal blood.

JACQUES: *(Laughing in disbelief.)* Why the devil would you want to do that?

EDRED: Because I was certain that I was the *last free* Englishman left alive, and I wanted to remember forever the *taste* of my lost inheritance.

ELIZABETH: But how could you be the last Englishman?

EDRED: For the tragic reason that all the other survivors of the Battle of Sanguelac became William the Conqueror's vassals, so they were forced to speak French. Then the Normans made the rest of the population into their slaves. Hence my age-old problem with the Froggies. But then the millions and millions of *un*numbered dead are the true history of the world, aren't they? Though I'm sure, Jacques, that your Upper Sixth teacher gave you a rather more anodyne version of history, didn't she?

JACQUES: *(Pouring himself some wine.)* OK, OK, I've got to admit your mind-reading act is pretty cool but…

EDRED: *(Overriding him.)* Then, later, when I went on the Crusades, I had the pleasure of sucking the blood of Moslems as well as Christians. Indeed, it was as the result of my dining on Moslems that I developed this penchant for garlic.

JACQUES: Oh come off it, everyone knows vampires hate garlic.

EDRED: Sorry, but that's just more of that melodramatic 'Dracula' nonsense. Whereas a *real,* thousand-year-old vampire, like me, regards garlic as the most deliciously-sensual stimulant. Which is why I first acquired the taste for it during the Crusades because it was continually oozing out of all those dying Muslims' pores, so I just felt compelled to go on drinking pints and pints of their succulent, spicy blood. As a result, ever since, I've always found that Christians taste rather bland. 'Fact it was while I was on the Crusades that I met the great Moslem leader, Saladin. Yes, and unlike Richard Coeur de Lyon, Saladin was a real gentleman, which is why he and I always got on admirably. In fact I never even felt the need to bite him, so I left him with his jugular intact. Mind, the reason for that was, that whenever there was a pause in the battle with the Crusaders, Salad – that's what I used to call him – well, Salad, like the real gentleman he was, would generously provide ices and fresh horses for all his enemies, so that they could all go on fighting against him with renewed vigour. Which is a damn sight more than Genghis Khan ever did for his enemies, when I was with him, and he was rampaging around Asia with his Golden Horde. 'Fact Genghis' favourite saying was; 'Let us kill all the males that are taller than our axles, Edred, and we'll take the rest as slaves'.

ELIZABETH: *(Laughing.)* And did you bite Genghis?

EDRED: Absolutely not! He smelt of boiled yak's milk. *(ELIZABETH continues to laugh.)* I know, I know. But unbelievable as it sounds, Elizabeth, everything that I'm telling you, it *really* did happen to me.

ELIZABETH: *(Still laughing.)* You are a bit…different, aren't you, Edred?

EDRED: That is the understatement of the Millennium, my dear.

JACQUES: Yes, Edred, and now you've got this very unvampire 'love of garlic', I suppose you don't even shrivel up if you're exposed to sunlight, either.

EDRED: Of course I don't. As I keep telling you, Jacques; fear of garlic and sunlight is all part of that fallacious 'Dracula' myth, concocted by that Victorian stage-manager-cum-pseudo-novelist, Bram Stoker. So, not only do I love garlic, but hot sunshine to me is a genuine tonic. 'Fact the sun is the only thing that really warms up my thousand-year-old bones.

JACQUES: Yeah, but what if I hammered a wooden stake right through your heart? That'd finish you off for good and all, wouldn't it?

EDRED: No, I've had stakes hammered into me numerous times over the centuries. But as I have no heart, there's nothing the stakes can hurt, is there? So I just pull 'em out, and almost immediately my chest and ribcage seal themselves up again. Then, once more, it's onwards and downwards. That's why there's absolutely nothing that you – or anyone – can do me to me that will harm me in any way. Not even *real, tangible* dangers could touch me – like the global bubonic plague, the Black Death. That didn't kill me, either. And the Black Death lasted the best part of a hundred years, and yet 25 million people, a third of Medieval Europe's population, died of it. But curiously, they all died in much the same way – like millions of over-fed, gluttonous vampires.

JACQUES: How could millions of people with the plague die like 'gluttonous vampires'?

EDRED: Because they all spent the last three agonising days of their lives vomiting up pints of their own blood until they all but drowned in it. But *I* was totally immune, and went on living through it all. Even though, for most of those abhorrent years, I had plague-ridden rats swarming all over me as I drank the diseased blood of the countless, corrupting dead.

ELIZABETH: Why'd you want to do something so gross?

EDRED: I hoped their blood would poison me, and then, at last, I would die. And that would've been bliss.

ELIZABETH: So, at times, you *have* wanted to…die, then?

EDRED: Latterly, more often than not.

JACQUES: But why ever would you want to die?

EDRED: If *you* had had the misfortune to live even a *fraction* as long as *I* have, Jacques, death would also seem to you to be the greatest of blessings. In fact, as the result of my *not-*dying, I suffered several decades of almost total insanity. So during the Middle Ages, I spent most of my time in my own private Halls of Bedlam. Mind, over the centuries, I have watched whole communities become *equally* insane – when they have all turned into deranged vampire-*hunters.*

ELIZABETH: How could whole communities have become deranged?

EDRED: Because in their vampire-hunting paranoia, people from the towns and villagers all over Europe insanely dug up their *own* relations, and their neighbours' dead bodies. And when they saw blood seeping from the mouth or the nose of one of the corpses, they believed they had disinterred a vampire. Their suspicions were further compounded because…perhaps one of the cadaver's eyes was open, and also it may have had a ruddy complexion. So then, in their fearful, mistaken frenzy, I've seen hundreds of panic-stricken villagers and townsfolk drive sharpened stakes into the corpses of their own relatives and friends.

JACQUES: Yeah, but they couldn't all be wrong.

ELIZABETH: 'Specially if there was blood seeping out of the corpse's mouth, and it had a ruddy complexion and an eye open. *(To JACQUES.)* Well, when *that* happened; surely seeing is believing, right?

EDRED: On the contrary. When a recently-buried corpse is disinterred, it can often appear to be what it isn't.

JACQUES: Oh come off it. A corpse is still just a corpse, isn't it?

EDRED: Yes, but in the confines of its coffin, Jacques, a corpse can swell up, and look ruddy and bloated as all the gases from its decomposition gather inside the corpse's torso. Then the increased pressure from the gasses can cause blood to ooze out of the corpse's mouth and its nose. This makes the body look well-fed, and still living. Especially if one of its eyes also happens to be open, which is actually quite common. So as the blood continues to ooze between the corpse's incisors, that can easily convince the ignorant masses that they have just dug up a vampire who's had a couple of bloody pints too many.

ELIZABETH: Ugh!

EDRED: Indeed, because then, in horror and terror, the villagers dementedly hammer a stake into the swollen chest of the blood-dribbling corpse. And, as more of the accumulated gases pass over the corpse's vocal chords, they produce a groan-like noise in the corpse's throat that makes it sound as if it's still alive. Simultaneously other gasses gush up through the cadaver's vibrating rectum, and the villagers believe that the vampire is farting at them. So, now in total panic, they hammer the stake even harder into the corpse's chest, which makes the farting get louder and louder.

JACQUES: Now you're really taking the piss. Well, dribbling blood and groaning's one thing, but a farting vampire!

EDRED: I'm only telling you what countless ignorant people have believed throughout Europe over the centuries, Jacques. Which is why it was me who first coined the phrase; 'He's nothing but an old fart.' Talking of which, I did once have the pleasure of hearing the world's most gifted, *young* fart, Wolfgang Amadeus Mozart, in flatulent action. In fact, Wolfy was such a musical genius, he could fart up and down the scale with perfect pitch. But more seriously, even during the 18ᵗʰ century, there was a plethora of so-called vampire sightings throughout great swathes of Eastern Europe, when innumerable graves were dug up, and hundreds of townsfolk ran amok around their local cemeteries, driving stakes through the hearts of their dead relatives and neighbours.

ELIZABETH: Unbelievable.

EDRED: Yes, and this hysterical delirium, known as 'The Eighteenth Century Vampire Controversy', lasted for the best part of a whole generation. But then, even in the Twentieth Century, there have also been periodic bouts of vampire hysteria. What's more, the last notable vampiric furore took place as recently as March 1970, and here in England, on Friday 13ᵗʰ, in Highgate Cemetery.

JACQUES: *(Ironic.)* Yeah, it had to be in Highgate Cemetery on Friday the bloody 13ᵗʰ, didn't it?

ELIZABETH: Oh come off it, babes! Highgate's a nice place, so you don't have to be so sarky 'bout it. I used to live there when I was little.

JACQUES: So what can you remember about it that's so 'nice' if you were only 'little'?

ELIZABETH: *(Upset.)* I remember enough things.

EDRED: I'm sure you do, Elizabeth.

ELIZABETH: *(After blowing her nose.)* Don't want to talk about it! All I know is Highgate was a helluva lot better than living with my aunt in bloody Rickmansworth.

JACQUES: Yeah, well, *we* used to have to live in Whitechapel, and that was a total shit hole, so I'm glad we moved to Ricky.

EDRED: You surprise me. Considering Whitechapel's got an infinitely richer history than 'Ricky'. Plus, of course, you've always got the chance of meeting up with the ghost of the Ripper in Whitechapel. And as for Highgate, Elizabeth, I agree with you. What's more, if you'd been alive in 1970, you'd've had the dubious privilege of meeting *me* there – because, of course, *I* was the Highgate Vampire. And, indeed, on Friday 13th, March 1970, as a result of some hyped-up publicity on ITV, suddenly there were large numbers of vampire-hunters from all over London, who went charging around Highgate Cemetery, clutching stakes and cloves of garlic, and they were all chasing after… *(EDRED swishes his cloak and grins.)* …yours truly. Naturally, the fruitcake vampire hunters never caught me. But it still made me laugh so much that I had to retire to the local priest's coffin to recover. So much so, I stayed in and around Highgate for the next twenty years or so, playing the predatory will-o'-the-wisp around Karl Marx's tomb – where, as chance would have it, I met someone who was, momentarily, very dear to me.

ELIZABETH: Who was that?

EDRED: And she had such a radiant smile. Indeed, if I'd had a heart, it might well have broken it.

ELIZABETH: So who was she, then?

EDRED: She was a true lover of the Living Dead.

JACQUES: She was a what?

ELIZABETH: Yes, Edred. Why can't you ever say anything just like… straight?

EDRED: Because the world is crooked, my dear. So during my infinite life, I have been constantly metamorphosing myself to conform with its crookedness. Which induced me, in one of my earliest bizarre incarnations, to turn myself into a rampaging ramanga.

JACQUES: Whatever's a ramanga when it's home?

EDRED: It's the Madagascan word for 'vampire'. And while I was this ramanga, I not only drank litres of blood from the Betsileo people, but I was so out of my skull at the time that – for dessert – I ate the nail-clippings of all their nobles.

ELIZABETH: Ugh! That's so rank.

EDRED: I agree. And when, at last, I recovered my wits, then I knew for certain that I was eternally damned. Even though *my* blood-thirsty exploits were as nothing compared to the Mass-Murderers in history. So as there was no imminent prospect of me dying, I decided it was my duty to witness, and record, the truly-horrific exploits of the World's Mass-Murderers because – unlike me – *they* have made life a continuous living-hell for mankind.

JACQUES: Oh give us a break. How could you possibly get right round the world to do that?

EDRED: In those days I could fly.

JACQUES: So where's your bat's wings now, then? Have they just shrivelled up and dropped off?

EDRED: In a manner of speaking – because I no longer have any use for them. Everything I ever needed to see, I've already seen innumerable time. And if my memory serves – and now, I must admit, I do occasionally have the odd Senior moment – but I think I'm right in recollecting that the very last time I flew – was on Concorde, which proved to be an unnecessarily-noisy, Frogified experience. But whenever I've needed to fly in the past, my aeronautical skills have enabled me to materialise at the elbow of…well, for instance; the Dominican, Torquemada, when he was the Grand Master of the Inquisition. Then I watched him torture all and sundry in the name of Christ His Saviour – because His Saviour certainly didn't bother to save any of his victims.

ELIZABETH: You really watched Torquemada torture…?

JACQUES: *(Overriding her.)* 'Course he didn't!

EDRED: And I stood beside King Ferdinand and Queen Isabella while they presided over the burning of 2000 so-called heretics. Also I was in Rome when Pope Paul sent his Inquisitors to every Catholic country to ensure that Christian burnings went on and on and on. Yet, in retrospect, hard as it is to believe; *those* were the *good* times.

ELIZABETH: *(Incredulous.)* They were 'the good times'?

EDRED: Absolutely. Because then along came Ivan the Terrible – and as a result of his massacres, the vast accumulation of corpses caused several Russian rivers to burst their banks. But still – as I say – compared to the terrors that were to be unleashed in later centuries – Ivan wasn't 'terrible' at all. He was just typical of most despots, before and since, who have all justified their mass murders by claiming that they were merely trying 'to strengthen' their *own* nations. Yet the only thing that Ivan and all those other 'Great Nationalists' have ever really succeeded in creating is Mass Organised Terror that has filled the world's graveyards to overflowing. Yet I wasn't always up to my nostrils in other people's blood and guts.

JACQUES: You could've fooled me.

EDRED: *(Smiling.)* Oh I don't have to try, Jacques, to do that. Come here, Elizabeth.

JACQUES: Don't!

ELIZABETH: I'll be fine. *(She crosses to EDRED and stares into his eyes. Then she whispers to EDRED in disbelief.)* So…you even knew…*him*, then?

JACQUES: Who's 'him'?

ELIZABETH: Edred, you know who I'm talking about, don't you?

EDRED: *(Amused.)* You'll be saying next, Elizabeth, that you can read my mind.

ELIZABETH: Only when you want me to. And you obviously do now. So was he like…awesome?

JACQUES: What dumbo are you wittering on about now?

ELIZABETH: William Shakespeare was many things, babes, but he certainly wasn't a 'dumbo.' What's more, Edred met him. *(To EDRED.)* Didn't you?

JACQUES: Oh come off it, Edred. You never met Shakespeare!

EDRED: I more than met him. I slept with him.

ELIZABETH: You didn't?

EDRED: But I never bit him.

ELIZABETH: Well, I s'ppose that's something.

EDRED: Oh I'm always very selective about whom I bite, Elizabeth. And Sweet Willy – which is what I used to call him – was far too exceptional a genius to wander around with holes in his throat. But Sweet Willy wasn't that extraordinary as a man, you understand. Indeed, I found him to be quite average between the sheets. But as I knew that he was destined to be the greatest poet-cum-dramatist who's ever lived, whenever we were in bed together, I always controlled myself, and I only licked Sweet Willy's… quill. But then, I was in one of my more benevolent, switch-hitting periods.

JACQUES: Are you still like…a switch-hitter, then?

EDRED: If the boys are pretty enough. And *you* are, Jacques.

JACQUES: Bugger me!

EDRED: I will if you want me to.

JACQUES: No, you bloody won't!

EDRED: Don't worry, Jacques-anory, I was only half teasing. But to get back to Willy. In return for me just licking him, I persuaded Willy to let me create the role of Macbeth.

JACQUES: That's your biggest load of turds yet! Everyone knows that Richard Burbage played Macbeth in front of James the First at Hampton Court.

EDRED: You're so wrong, Jacques. See, I was *there*, remember, and during that time, Burbage was drunk as a skunk for weeks on end in a Cheapside brothel.

JACQUES: Then why did Holinshed say Burbage was the first Macbeth? And he's a genuine historian.

EDRED: Because I'm not just the oldest of the Living Dead, Jacques, I'm also the world's greatest Shape-Shifter; so I made myself *look* and *sound* like Burbage. Besides, Holinshed was very short-sighted, and he was all but deaf in both of his wax-filled ears.

ELIZABETH: That's just so amazingly cool.

JACQUES: If you believe that, babes, you'll believe anything.

ELIZABETH: No, the reason it's so cool, Edred, is 'cause *I'm* about to give *my* Lady Macbeth soon myself.

EDRED: I know. That's why I let you read a minuscule segment of my mind. Mind, unfortunately, when *I* was creating Macbeth in the original production, I had to make do with a pustular boy, by the name of Edmans, as my Lady Macbeth. Though I must say Edmans did have a perky codpiece and inviting buttocks.

JACQUES: Fuck a duck!

EDRED: Any time. But then I've found that ducks and boys have a lot in common. Yes, I know. I'm not what you'd call a 'politically-correct' vampire. And while we're on the subject of 'Macbeth', although I've always had a soft spot for 'Mackers' – mainly because of its plenitude of corpses – yet I still infinitely prefer 'Titus Andronicus' as that is a truly wall-to-wall blood-fest. So I absolutely adored playing Titus. I especially savoured the moment when I served up Queen Tamara's dismembered children – to her – in a huge, steaming pie. Indeed, it's the principle reason that I had to *re*-write a lot of the lines in 'Macbeth' for poor old Willy. You see, so many of Willy's lines lacked real…well, 'bite'. Also I knew that that other shirt-lifter, King James, would keenly relish hearing some sexy, blood-boltered imagery on the first night.

ELIZABETH: You saying you like…re-wrote some of Shakespeare's lines?

EDRED: Absolutely. And I wrote and inspired vast chunks of Christopher Marlowe's work, too. Mind, Chris liked to be called 'Kit', so, of course, I always called him 'Kitty'.

JACQUES: Rubbish! There's no way you could've inspired Kitty…Kit Marlowe!

EDRED: Well, how else do you think Kitty came up with the idea of writing his diabolical 'Faustus'. Not to mention that loveable butcher, 'Tamberlaine the Great, Parts One and Two'. And, of course, we mustn't forget 'Edward II', who dies in incandescent ecstasy when Lightbourne shoves a red-hot poker up his bum. But then, of course – unlike Willy and me – Kitty only swung *one* way. So no wonder Kitty said; 'Anyone who doesn't love boys and tobacco, doesn't love life.'

ELIZABETH: Yes, but you still haven't told us *your* lines which you said you put into 'Macbeth'?

JACQUES: Oh, don't encourage him, for God's sake!

ELIZABETH: No, tell me, please, Edred!

EDRED: Well, naturally most of the blood-soaked lines in
'Macbeth' are mine – like…
…'This bloody piece of work;
And it will have blood;
They say blood will have blood;
And I am blood
Stepp'd in so far that, should I wade no more,
Returning were as tedious as go o'er,'
because I am 'the secret'st man of blood'.

And if that's not enough blood and gore for you,
my piece de resistance was;
'What bloody man is that?'
(Smiling.) Yes, and when you think about that line, it just
about sums me up, doesn't it?

ELIZABETH: Wish I'd been your Lady Macbeth, Edred.

JACQUES: Oh c'mon, you can't mean that, babes!

EDRED: You still can be my Lady Macbeth. *(EDRED gestures
ELIZABETH to join him.)* So…'Come…'

ELIZABETH: …'You spirits,
That tend on mortal thoughts, unsex me here,
And fill me, from the crown to the toe, top-full
Of direst cruelty!'

EDRED: 'Make thick my blood…'

ELIZABETH: You wrote that, too?

EDRED: *(Amused.)* Of course.

JACQUES: Bloody hell!

EDRED: Yes, Jacques, Hell is certainly sanguinary.

(EDRED indicates to ELIZABETH that she should continue acting.)

ELIZABETH: 'Make thick my blood;
Stop up the access and passage to remorse,
that no compunctious visitings of nature
Shake my fell purpose, nor keep peace between
The effect and it. Come to my woman's breasts…

(EDRED points to her breasts.)

EDRED: Yes, and very nice they are, too, my dear. But though
I do swing both ways, in your case, I…

ELIZABETH: *(Overriding him.)* It would be a helluva waste if
you didn't 'swing both ways', Edred. So like…what famous
women did you sleep with, then?

JACQUES: Knowing him, the Virgin Queen.

EDRED: Yes, actually I did sleep with Bawdy Bess, along, of course, with Essex, Raleigh and the rest of her Court.

ELIZABETH: Then there's nothing you don't know, Edred. *(Sexily to him.)* So…'Come to my woman's breasts'…

JACQUES: *(To EDRED.)* Now if you touch her, you creepy bastard, I'll…

ELIZABETH: *(Persisting, to EDRED.)* 'Come to my woman's breasts…'

(EDRED overrides her and applauds her.)

EDRED: Yes, yes, that was wonderfully acted, darling. But you don't need to go on. The rest of the speech any good actress can do. No, the real challenge for anyone playing Lady M. comes later, when Macduff rushes in and announces;
'O Banquo, Banquo! Our royal master's murder'd.'
And Lady M. responds with the immortal words…

ELIZABETH: *(Clutching her breasts and speaking with a sob in her voice.)* 'Woe! Alas!
What? In our house?'

(JACQUES bursts out laughing.)

ELIZABETH: You little shit!

EDRED: True, but Jacques does have a point, Lizzie, 'cause those lines of Lady M's *shouldn't* make one guffaw. What's more, I told Wee Willy Winkey that he should change Lady M's lines because I knew only too well that 'What? In our house?' would literally bring the house down. What's more, it did. 'Fact on the opening night, King Jamey the Sax laughed so much, I thought he was going to wet himself. But Willy was such a stubborn bugger, he refused to change anything. As a result, every poor actress has been lumbered with those risible words ever since.

JACQUES: OK, Edred, OK. You've had your bit of fun with
'Willy' and 'Kitty'. But you still haven't told us what *any* of
this has got to do with…

EDRED: *(Completing his question.)* …Your nightmares, right?

JACQUES: Right!

EDRED: I'm simply putting your forthcoming storm into
context, my friend – because when your answers come – as
they will now – you may well wish they hadn't.

ELIZABETH: Yeah, you're such a twat, Jacques! You laughed
at me just then to spoil everything. I was really enjoying
doing Lady Macbeth. And if I'd've gone on, I'm sure
Edred would have given me some valuable notes that
would've improved like…my interpretation.

*(ELIZABETH finishes off her goblet of wine, and then immediately
starts to refill her goblet.)*

JACQUES: Look, don't drink any more, babes. Not with him
letching at you.

ELIZABETH: For God's sake, stop telling me what to do! I'm
sick of it.

EDRED: Do you like cricket, Jacques?

JACQUES: I do, actually. But what's cricket got to do with…?

EDRED: *(Overriding him.)* Everything; because I was there
when cricket was first invented, so I'm the only cricket-
loving vampire in existence. What's more, I was the very
first umpire. And, of course, 'umpire' is just a mis-spelling
for 'vampire'. Naturally it was *my* idea to make the ball red.
But then I've always had a penchant for everything that's
red and runny. *(He pours JACQUES, ELIZABETH and himself
some more wine.)* Though I must admit, I did find the French
Revolution, with those old blood-thirsty women knitting
beside Madame Guillotine, a little too red in the tooth
even for me. But that was just the beginning of Totalitarian
Terror.

JACQUES: Yeah, but where the hell's all this leading us?

ELIZABETH: Just let him finish, Jacques. We're getting close.

EDRED: Indeed we are, because a new reign of even greater Terror returned with Lenin and his Bolshevik Revolution. Then, of course, Hitler created his own horrific terror, which was far worse than the Russian Revolution. But alongside the Fuhrer was Stalin, who murdered 30 million which was even more than Hitler killed. Then there was Chairman Mao, with his 70 million dead, which was twice as many as Stalin.

JACQUES: OK, OK, so the Twentieth Century was nothing but a giant butcher's yard. So bloody what?

EDRED: So – during the very 'bloody' Twentieth Century, Jacques, there was a Global Hemoclysm, which took the lives of well-over 150 million, totally-innocent people.

ELIZABETH: Hemoclysm?

EDRED: It's the Greek word for 'blood flood.' And in the entire history of the world, there's never been such a flood of blood as was spilt in the last century. Yet from the *Earth's* point of view, Hitler, Stalin, Mao and their ilk, didn't kill anywhere near *enough* people, did they?

ELIZABETH: How can you say that?

JACQUES: Yeah, that's just sick!

EDRED: Yes, the Earth *is* sick of having far too many people on it, who are continually polluting it and causing climate change, which will soon reduce the Earth into being one third desert and two-thirds ocean. When that happens, there'll scarcely be any human survivors. So the only way Mankind will survive on Earth is if it is fortunate enough to lose over *three-quarters* of its ever-increasing population in some new form of cataclysmic blood-flood.

ELIZABETH: You really believe that?

EDRED: I no longer know what I believe – about anything – because my world has been nothing but blood. But then *you* are both covered in blood in your dreams, aren't you?

ELIZABETH: That's not true!

EDRED: You may lie to me, Elizabeth, but if you want your nightmares to cease, you must not behave like all those mega butchers of the past who refused to face the truth about their monstrous actions. No, instead – unlike them – you must stop lying to yourself and confront the horrific truth about yourself.

ELIZABETH: I'm not lying, you shitty bastard!

EDRED: *(Clapping her.)* Bravo! Bravissimo, Elizabeth! Or should I say…'Erzebet'? Because your scatological outburst was far more reminiscent of Countess Erzsebet's infamous temper-tantrums.

JACQUES: Countess who?

EDRED: Yes, we're nearly there now, Jacques. *(To ELIZABETH.)* So – Erzebet – other than accidentally biting your tongue yesterday – when was the last time you actually *drank* blood?

ELIZABETH: I've never drunk blood!

EDRED: Not even in the dungeon of your nightmares, Erzebet?

JACQUES: For God's sake, just leave her alone, and stop calling her that!

EDRED: Surely that's why you came to me, Erzebet?

ELIZABETH: Yes, why'd you keep calling me 'Erzebet'? When you know my name's 'Elizabeth'.

EDRED: Because 'Erzebet' is Hungarian for 'Elizabeth'. And in one of your previous lives, you were Countess Erzebet Bathor.

JACQUES: *(To ELIZABETH.)* Don't listen to him, babes. He's trying to pull some reincarnation garbage on you. *(To EDRED.)* Aren't you?

EDRED: I easily could hypnotise you, Erzebet, and prove to you who you were.

JACQUES: I bet! Anything to get into her pants!

ELIZABETH: Look, will you just shut up a minute, Jacques?

JACQUES: Why the hell should I?

ELIZABETH: 'Cause the name of… Erzebet…Bathor…well, now it's like…ringing some sorta…bell inside my head.

JACQUES: No, no, like I keep telling you, babes; that bastard's just screwing with your mind, so he can screw *you!*

ELIZABETH: No, no, Jacques. Edred is trying to help me. Don't you understand that?

EDRED: Yes, I am trying to help you. But first you must return to that dank, blood-stained cellar in your nightmares, Erzebet, and you must remember everything you did there because only then will you…

ELIZABETH: *(Overriding him.)* No, please, don't make me go there!

JACQUES: Yes, that's more'n enough, you sicko! Now gimme the key, 'cause me and Lizzie are getting outta here now!

EDRED: Certainly. *(EDRED takes the key out of his pocket, but he ignores JACQUES' outstretched hand. Instead he places the key in ELIZABETH's hand. Then EDRED folds her fingers around the key.)* Now run off into the dark, Erzebet, where you'll continue to embrace your interminable nights of blood.

JACQUES: Yes, come on, babes, let's go!

(ELIZABETH shakes her head at JACQUES. Then she whispers to EDRED.)

ELIZABETH: Edred…

EDRED: Yes, Erzebet?

ELIZABETH: If I…well, if I like face my nightmares, can you really… stop me having them again?

EDRED: So you *do* believe me?

ELIZABETH: Yeah…

JACQUES: No, don't listen to him, babes. There's nothing he can do to help you, so let's go! *(EDRED sits, and ELIZABETH moves closer to him.)* Babes!

EDRED: So now you do accept that you were Erzebet Bathor in one of your reincarnations?

JACQUES: Now don't start all that reincarnation crap again. 'Cause no one believes in it.

EDRED: Not in the West, they don't. But, with the exception of the Moslems, most believers in the East take reincarnation for granted, and they make up a large proportion of the world's population. And as the Tibetan Buddhists say; 'If you die with a peaceful mind, you'll experience a fortunate rebirth. But if you die with a disturbed mind because of what you have done in your violent life – Erzebet – then you will experience an horrific re-birth.'

ELIZABETH: You saying that…well, *that's* what's happened to me?

EDRED: Yes, and the Mahapuranas were even more graphic about it.

JACQUES: The Mara-whats?

EDRED: Mahapuranas were very early Hindu writings. On the subject of reincarnation they state that 'the murderer of a virgin becomes a leper; if you commit illicit intercourse, you are reborn as a eunuch, and, of course, if you're an eater of meat, your flesh becomes very red'…

JACQUES: *(Overriding him.)* So with the amount of blood you've drunk, Edred, you should've turned into a bloody beetroot!

EDRED: *(Laughing.)* Touché – as the Froggies say. Indeed, that mordantly-mischievous quip of yours is almost worthy of a vampire.

ELIZABETH: Edred, do you really believe in like… reincarnation, then?

EDRED: I believe in everything, and nothing – because my endless life has disproved everything, and proved nothing. But as I live most of the time in infinite Hell, I know only too well what you are suffering now, Erzebet.

ELIZABETH: It's true. If I keep having these horrible dreams, I'm going to have…well, I'm going to have some kind of… well, like nervous breakdown.

JACQUES: Yes, Lizzie, but if you stay here much longer arguing the toss with this tosser, we're both going to end up in the local nuthouse.

ELIZABETH: Look, stop being a twat, Jacques. I need to know the truth. And so do *you*! What's more, in your heart, you know you do.

JACQUES: *(Gesticulating at EDRED.)* The truth's the last thing you'll get from this sick freak!

ELIZABETH: You're the one's that's sick, Jacques. Or why are all your dreams so violent and full of blood?

JACQUES: God knows! But there's nothing anyone can do 'bout 'em.

ELIZABETH: Well, *you've* got to do something about 'em, Jacques, 'cause for the last three nights you've been laughing in your sleep about killing and spilling blood, and…twice you've almost strangled me!

JACQUES: *(Slumping into a pew.)* You never said I…

ELIZABETH: *(Overriding him.)* I did! But you wouldn't listen. You just stormed off. Then last night in our tent, you lunged at me in your sleep and clamped your hands 'round my throat. Then you ripped one of the metal tent pegs out of the ground and tried to stab me with it. And if I hadn't kicked you in the balls, you could've…well, you could've stabbed me in…my womb.

JACQUES: I can't take any more of this! Now gimme the key.

ELIZABETH: Here, take the key. *(She gives JACQUES the key.)* But when you've unlocked the door, before you run off, make sure you leave the key *in* it.

JACQUES: Aren't you coming with me, then?

ELIZABETH: No. Why should I?

JACQUES: Look, please, come with me, babes!

ELIZABETH: And don't come back for me 'till you're ready to face up to the truth 'bout *yourself.*

JACQUES: You can't possibly stay here with this nutcase, babes.

ELIZABETH: I can. 'Cause it was *you* who tried to strangle me, 'babes', not *him.* So if there's a nutcase 'round here, it's *you!* Yeah, and I know the reason why you act like a maniac in your sleep.

JACQUES: No, you don't. You haven't a clue. Anymore than *I* have.

ELIZABETH: I've got more than a clue. See, the reason you go crazy in your dreams, Jacques, is 'cause *I'm* going to Cambridge, while *you're* going nowhere. 'Cause you didn't get good 'nough grades to go to Uni. You spent too much time on that stupid project on the Supernatural. So now I'm going to be having a fantastic time in Jesus College, and you're going to be stuck in Ricky, which we both know's a total dump. So you'll probably end up unemployed and going off your head. And the thought of that makes you like envy the cool life I'm going to be having without you. And deep-down, Jacques, you know *it's* the truth. That's why you keep attacking me in your sleep.

JACQUES: No, no, you got it all wrong, babes. My nightmares have nothing to do with that.

EDRED: Then what *have* they got to do with, Jacques?

JACQUES: I don't know. Yet they have nothing to do with *her*. But *you're* the reason she's turned against me! You've been screwing with her mind, so now she thinks she doesn't love me, or…need me, or even care for me anymore. And I'm sick to death of everything!

ELIZABETH: So why don't you just take a long walk around the graveyard? And don't come back 'till you want to face up to the truth 'bout yourself, 'cause that's the only way you're gonna sort out your rotten life.

JACQUES: *(Furious and close to tears.)* Oh go to Hell! Both of you!

(JACQUES grabs his rucksack and storms off with it.)

ELIZABETH: *(Calling after him.)* And don't slam the door.

EDRED: You're right not to want to go with him.

ELIZABETH: *(Suddenly unsure.)* Am I?

EDRED: And Jacques is right when he says you don't love him – because you don't, do you?

ELIZABETH: Dunno… It comes…and goes. But since he's started to…well, attack me in his sleep, there's not been much to…love.

EDRED: So you prefer to stay here with me?

ELIZABETH: Yeah. But only 'cause I need to know the truth about… well, 'bout what's happening to me.

EDRED: You're not afraid of me, then?

ELIZABETH: I am. Well, you still…unnerve me, but…

EDRED: *(Completing her thought.)* …But you're young, so you enjoy flirting with danger. You even find evil seductive.

ELIZABETH: I don't!

EDRED: Part of you does, or you wouldn't have risked coming to find me. Yes, and that part of you feels immortal. It makes you believe you won't suffer any fatal consequences for anything you do.

(There is a distant flash of lightning.)

ELIZABETH: Perhaps you're right. I dunno anymore. 'Fact I'm not sure what I believe about…well, 'bout anything anymore. All I know is, nothing can be as bad as my nightmares. 'Cause these last few weeks…in my dreams I seem to be…well, I seem to be part of such…cruel and… rank things that they're like… *(There is another lighting flash.)* …well, they're like flashes of lightning that have…blood on them.

EDRED: That only confirms in a previous incarnation that you were the Countess Erzebet Bathor – because she bathed in her victims' blood, and she was cruel beyond thought.

ELIZABETH: What did this…Erzebet Bathor do that was so horrible?

EDRED: In her numerous killing sprees, the Countess exhibited such a frenzied blood-lust that she would even have put a vampire to shame. But she was not a vampire. Although she was compared to Vlad the Impaler.

ELIZABETH: But how could any woman…even this Countess kill like Vlad the Impaler did? 'Cause I read he had thousands of people impaled on wooden stakes.

EDRED: Indeed he did. But Bathor didn't kill thousands. No, it was the *way* she tortured and murdered dozens of girls and young women, over a period of twenty years, in the dungeon of her castle at Cachtice, that has earned her the infamous title of 'The Blood Countess'. That is why, Erzebet, you must confront your nightmares. And the only way you can do that is to tell me what cruel and vile things you have done in your dreams.

ELIZABETH: Well…in some of my…worst dreams, I seem to be…like you said…down in a dark dungeon where… young girls are chained to the walls. Then I've…well, I've been like…burning and mutilating their hands and…their faces, and even their…their… Then I bite the flesh off other girl's faces…and claw their breasts, and then I drink their blood. But sometimes when I've dreamt I've done these…rank things, I like…force myself awake. Then I rush out of my bedroom so I can throw up. I have *to try to* make myself clean again. See, I know I'm *not* like that! I've never done nothing like that, and I never could. So when did this evil woman live…and where?

EDRED: Erzebet Bathor was a 17th Century Hungarian Countess, who was arrested – and tried in absentia – for killing and mutilating over 600 hundred girls and young women in her castle dungeon, with the assistance of her three equally-sadistic servants. But more importantly, in *your* case, I'm right in saying, aren't I? – that during these last two weeks, when you've been camping with Jacques – your dreams have been totally different. Indeed, in some of your latest nightmares, *you* have been very close to death *yourself,* haven't you?

ELIZABETH: *(Nodding.)* It's true…in some of my…well, my more recent dreams, I'm not in that horrible dungeon, but I'm in a different part of the castle. And it's like…well, it's like I'm imprisoned there. Yes, I seem to have been… cemented-up behind these thick walls. Then I keep kind of prowling up and down behind these walls like a caged animal, 'cause I feel terribly guilty about what I've done to those girls. Yet in my prison behind these walls, although I desperately want to die, I can't. I *can't* die! 'Fact, in my dreams, I'm like…well, I'm like *you* must be all the time, Edred.

EDRED: Yes, but *un*like me, you *did* die, Erzebet. And on the 21ˢᵗ of August, in the year 1614, you were found dead in your castle, surrounded by several plates of food that only the rats were feasting on. But these more-recent images of you being walled-up as the imprisoned Countess Erzebet, they only come to you once or twice a week, don't they? Because now, in your dreams, you are the torturer only very occasionally. What's more, since you've been sleeping in the tent with Jacques, your very latest nightmares have been filled with images of *you* being tortured, and often in the most horrific ways.

ELIZABETH: It's true. But how can you know all…?

EDRED: *(Overriding her.)* I'll come to that. So in your most recent dreams, *you* are now the one who is the terrified, cowering victim – and you're the one who's being mutilated, aren't you?

ELIZABETH: *(Near to tears.)* Yes.

EDRED: And the reason for that is; in reincarnation, what goes around, comes around. So you are no longer the torturing Blood Countess. No, now you're like one of her dying victims. But it's not the Countess who is nightly torturing you to death, is it?

ELIZABETH: No. But the last three nights, though I'm suffering horribly in my dreams, and my blood is just like…flooding out of me, yet I still can't seem to die. Even though he slashes open my throat, and stabs my stomach, and he… cuts bits out of my face, and off my…breasts, and then he thrusts his knife into my…my…

(Now distraught ELIZABETH breaks off.)

EDRED: Yet you still can't see his face, can you?

ELIZABETH: No, his face is always…hidden.

EDRED: Then… let us see him together.

ELIZABETH: How?

EDRED: Kiss me.

ELIZABETH: What?

EDRED: Kiss me. You know you want to.

ELIZABETH: No!

EDRED: Yes, you do. From the moment I touched your hand, and stroked your neck, you have wanted to kiss me. Nearly as much as you have ached for *me* to kiss *you*. And you know this is true. So…kiss me.

ELIZABETH: If I…do; will I then understand how…well, you know so much about me?

EDRED: Yes. And I will also learn certain things that I suspect, but I'm not fully sure of yet.

ELIZABETH: So there are things 'bout me you *don't* know, then?

EDRED: *(Nodding.)* And there always will be.

ELIZABETH: Then if I kiss you, I've…well, I've like nothing to lose, have I?

EDRED: Except yourself.

ELIZABETH: *(Close to tears.)* Oh…at this moment, Edred, that could be just so wonderful.

EDRED: So…kiss me.

(ELIZABETH nods, then she crosses to him. EDRED remains motionless. ELIZABETH moves even closer to him, inviting him to kiss her. But he shakes his head.)

EDRED: No. *You* must kiss me.

(ELIZABETH hesitates, then she offer hers lips to him again. EDRED still remains motionless, so ELIZABETH kisses him passionately, and he responds in kind.

Then abruptly ELIZABETH lurches away from him as if she has received an electric shock. EDRED smiles knowingly.)

ELIZABETH: It's not true!

EDRED: You know it is.

ELIZABETH: And *you* are….

EDRED: *(Overriding her.)* Yes. And I'll prove it to you. But before I do, it's imperative that you comprehend the enormity of what your very latest nightmares are telling you needs to be done.

ELIZABETH: No, I want the proof now!

EDRED: But if you don't go along with what I propose, Elizabeth, I cannot guarantee to save you.

ELIZABETH: Save me from what?

EDRED: From something fatal happening to you.

ELIZABETH: You're…serious, aren't you?

EDRED: Very.

ELIZABETH: And if I listen to what you like propose, and then I agree to go along with it, then you promise you'll give me the proof that….?

EDRED: *(Overriding her.)* Once you have sworn on this Bible, yes.

(He picks up the Bible from the altar.)

ELIZABETH: *(In disbelief.)* But how can you hold the Bible like that? Well, doesn't it like…*do* anything to you?

EDRED: What should it do to me? *(Realising and laughing.)* Oh yes, of course, you think – because I'm a vampire – that my holding the Bible should instantly reduce me to a pile of flaming ash. But as I keep telling you, Elizabeth, that's just more of Bram Stoker's 'Dracula' faeces. In fact the very opposite is true. Not only do I find the Bible to be completely harmless, but I often read it when I'm in need of a good laugh. Well, for a start, *I* make Old Methuselah in Genesis look like a spring chicken, don't I? *(He strokes the crucifix.)* As for crucifixes, I just adore stroking *them*, too. So, I reiterate, there's absolutely nothing that can terminate my hellish existence. Oh I know you think *your* nightmares are horrific, my dear, but they only torment you when you go to sleep. Whereas *I* can never sleep, so my world is comprised of a thousand years of wall-to-wall nightmares, with no end to them in sight.

ELIZABETH: When you put it like that, it's…well, it's so horrible.

EDRED: Yes. But now, for once in my interminable life, suddenly and unexpectedly, I find I want to do something that's… *(With an ironic laugh.)* …well, that's worthwhile.

ELIZABETH: Like what?

EDRED: I want to save you – from yourself. And I haven't done anything like that for anyone. Not for a very long time.

ELIZABETH: You really mean that, don't you?

EDRED: Yes, but this can only be accomplished, Elizabeth, if you swear on this Bible that you will answer my questions honestly, and then you will let me do what has to be done, so that I can save you.

ELIZABETH: And then you'll give me the proof that you are what I felt when I…well, when I kissed you.

EDRED: I promise.

(ELIZABETH approaches the altar. As she puts her hand on the Bible, there is a shimmer of lightning, followed by a distant thunder growl as the summer storm returns.)

ELIZABETH: Then I swear – on this Bible – that I'll try to go along with…well, with what you want to do for me.

EDRED: You'll only try?

ELIZABETH: Well, without knowing exactly what you intend to do, I'd be stupid to promise you anything more, wouldn't I?

EDRED: *(With an approving smile.)* Yes, yes, you will do well in life, Elizabeth. Given the shadow of a chance.

ELIZABETH: Then give me the chance.

(There is a vivid lightning flash, followed by more thunder.)

EDRED: Then answer me truthfully. In your latest dreams, when you are the tortured victim, do you still claim that you don't recognise the face of the man with the scalpel?

ELIZABETH: Yes. But how'd you know he's got a scalpel? I just thought it was like…well, like a knife with a long blade.

EDRED: No, it's a scalpel. But you're being untruthful when you say you don't recognise the man who is torturing you.

ELIZABETH: But I don't! See, he always has a strange…old-fashioned hat pulled right down over his eyes. And the bottom half of his face is covered with a kind of…scarf. So even when he drags me out from under the lamplight into the dark alley, I still can't see much of his face.

EDRED: Yes, he drags you out from under the *lamp*light – not from under the *electric* streetlights – because you are wearing a crinoline, aren't you? And your dress is spattered with your own blood. *(There is another crackle of lightning.)* But even as more of your blood seeps onto the muddy cobblestones, he still continues his surgical butchery. Then, momentarily, he pauses, doesn't he? Before he raises the scalpel above his head….

ELIZABETH: Yes! Then he slashes the knife down and…and, God help me, he…well, he…he…

(She trails off, fighting back her tears.)

EDRED: Say it.

ELIZABETH: He rips out my…womb, and then he… disembowels me. But I still can't die! Yet he goes on laughing at my pain…laughing and stabbing and…

(Lightning and thunder.)

EDRED: Yes, but even though you never see his face properly, *now* you know exactly *who* he is, don't you?

ELIZABETH: No! No, I don't!

EDRED: Oh yes, you do. And if we are to save your life, Elizabeth, you must tell me his name.

ELIZABETH: I don't know who he is!

EDRED: Come here, and I will give the proof you asked for.

(Thunder.)

ELIZABETH: No!

(Momentarily EDRED is illuminated by lightning.)

EDRED: And then I will make you Immortal – as one of the Living Dead.

ELIZABETH: *(Smiling.)* So you *do* want to…taste my blood?

EDRED: It's the only certain way to ensure that he will never hurt you anymore. And no one will. Ever.

ELIZABETH: And then I'll be like you, won't I?

EDRED: Yes. But, in truth, that is the very *last* thing I want.

ELIZABETH: Do you…really mean that?

EDRED: Yes.

ELIZABETH: Then I believe you. And I don't need any further proof.

(EDRED seems to shimmer in a lightning flash.)

EDRED: Ah…

ELIZABETH: But how did you…well, like…first meet her?

EDRED: She was in Highgate Cemetery, putting flowers on her uncle's grave. She dropped a lily, and I picked it up for her. As I returned the flower to her, she smiled at me so knowingly. She had such a radiant smile. In that regard, she was rather like you.

ELIZABETH: So then you treated her like…well, like you say you treated Shakespeare, and you didn't bite her?

EDRED: *(Amused.)* No, I didn't. However, unlike poor Sweet Willy, *she* was exceptional between the sheets. I'm sorry. I shouldn't have said that.

ELIZABETH: Was that…well, was that *all* there was to the time of…you both being together, then?

EDRED: No. You see, for once I was…well, I was almost… almost… *(EDRED trails off, which makes ELIZABETH smile.)* Why do you smile?

ELIZABETH: 'Cause it must be the first time *you've* ever been like lost for words.

EDRED: True, it doesn't happen very often. But I was… moved when she smiled at me, with such radiance, and so knowingly – because then, you see, I knew that she would die long before she should.

ELIZABETH: *(Suddenly fierce.)* But you said you didn't…?

EDRED: *(Quickly.)* She didn't die because of me, my dear. But her smile told me that she would die while she was still very young. And so that midsummer evening in the cemetery – because she was so redolent with life – I felt compelled to give her…something that would make her short life blossom 'till its end. And to ensure that this happened, I saw her several times more…

ELIZABETH: So *when* were you like…absolutely sure?

EDRED: About you?

ELIZABETH: Yes.

EDRED: I first sensed it when you told me that you were in Highgate when you were little, before you went to live with your aunt in Rickmansworth. Then when I stroked your neck, I knew there was something very different about you. But I was only absolutely certain when you kissed me. So come here…sweetheart.

ELIZABETH: Why?

EDRED: I want to hold you.

ELIZABETH: Wonderful. 'Cause now I want to live forever – with you. *(She crosses to EDRED, who enfolds her in his cloak. There is a shimmer of lightning and a crack of thunder as EDRED exposes ELIZABETH's neck. Then, seemingly, he prepares to sink his teeth into her flesh as they are illuminated by another vivid lightning flash. But EDRED shakes his head, and he moves away from her.)* Why've you pulled back? You must've done this like…a thousand times.

EDRED: Yes, but I've never done it to anyone I've…I've ever…

ELIZABETH: …Loved?

EDRED: Oh I've never really loved anyone. I doubt I ever will. But if I had a heart, *you* would surely touch it. Just as *she* did. So, instead, I will save you *from* yourself – with this.

(EDRED moves behind the altar. Then he produces a long knife from under the altar cloth. The knife glitters in a lightning flash…as the rest of the church starts to darken around him.)

ELIZABETH: What you going to do with…?

EDRED: *(Overriding her.)* In your nightmares he rips open your womb, and then he disembowels you with a blade such as this. So just speak his name, and I will free you from him forever.

ELIZABETH: It's not true, it's not…! *(She is silenced by a crack of thunder. Simultaneously EDRED places the knife on the altar as more menacing shadows gather around them.)* Why…is it growing so…dark in here?

(The church continues to grow darker.)

EDRED: Darkness is the only thing he understands, so it is the one certain way to induce his shadow-self to appear.

ELIZABETH: *(Pointing to the enveloping darkness.) You* are making the darkness fall, aren't you?

EDRED: Yes, but I'm only doing it for *you.* For *I* long for the dawn because – with me – it is always eternal night. Yes, and it was me that whispered in the almost-blind John Milton's ear as he wrote; 'Myself am Hell.'

ELIZABETH: And yet…if only for one moment, you have… well, you have felt some kind of love, haven't you? *(Suddenly distraught.)* For my mother.

EDRED: I certainly felt something for her. But then over the centuries, I have been a lover and a father countless times. *(Smiling ironically.)* Yet I've nearly always avoided meeting my arbitrary creations.

ELIZABETH: 'Till now. But then, of course, *I* didn't see very much of my mother… *(Fighting back her tears.)* …'cause she died of cancer when I was only four-and-a-half. It's why I was brought up by my aunt.

EDRED: Yes, and I foresaw your mother's death when she smiled at me so knowingly in the cemetery. But then…*you* are the 'something' that I created with her that….

ELIZABETH: *(Completing his thought.)* …'Made her short life blossom 'till its end.' *(Visibly moved EDRED nods.)* And now…because of the darkness you've brought down on us, I can hardly see you…Father.

EDRED: That's just as it should be.

(ELIZABETH crosses to EDRED, who is now enshrouded in shadows. But as EDRED enfolds ELIZABETH in his arms, the church is plunged into total darkness.)

ELIZABETH: Oh Father, please…

(In the enveloping darkness, there is a crash of thunder, followed by a lightning flash that briefly illuminates…the frenzied figure of JACQUES, who runs towards the altar, and snatches the knife from the altar-cloth. Then JACQUES lunges towards to ELIZABETH with the raised blade. But before JACQUES can reach her, once again the church is plunged into total darkness.)

JACQUES: *(Screaming in the darkness.)* She's mine! And if I can't have her, no one will!

(Then the most deafening peal of thunder cannonades over the church roof. Simultaneously there is a withering scream. Then silence.

A moment later, lightning flares over the altar to reveal…the now-hooded figure of EDRED, who is sitting on the altar steps, cradling the motionless figure of ELIZABETH in his arms.

The light that is emanating from EDRED slowly begins to suffuse the rest of the church, and we see that… JACQUES is lying in a crumpled heap on the flagstones. He is clutching the handle of the blood-stained knife that is protruding from his own chest, and he is very close to death.)

JACQUES: I heard…nearly everything, Lizzie. But I promise you, I'd…I'd never have…hurt you. Never! Yes, yes, I know I was the…face in your dreams… And it's true, in my…other life, I was…

EDRED: …Not Jacques – but as your father so appositely called you 'Jack', and it was 'Jack' who got the A Star in Biology, wasn't it?

JACQUES: But I'm only Jack the Ripper in my nightmares! Like *she* was the Blood Countess in hers. 'Cause neither of us could ever have done those terrible…evil things… Oh God…help me…

(JACQUES falls back dead.

Rhythmically stroking her neck, ELIZABETH gets to her feet uncertainly. Then she stops stroking her neck and she looks at her fingers. She sees that there is blood on her fingers.

Now terrified and shivering ELIZABETH crosses to JACQUES. Shaking her head in disbelief, she kneels by JACQUES' body. Then she turns to EDRED, who is still hooded and motionless.)

ELIZABETH: What are we…going to do now?

EDRED: Now that he's dead, you're free.

ELIZABETH: You killed him!

EDRED: Or he would have killed you.

ELIZABETH: I'm not free. I'll never be free! When the Police come, there'll…

EDRED: *(Overriding her.)* They'll do nothing.

(EDRED pushes back his hood. He has blood on his lips.)

EDRED: For there is nothing the Police – or anyone – can do now. To either of us. And as I have tasted your blood…I will never be alone again. Because now you, too, my dearest daughter, will, perforce, share with me the destiny of…everlasting life – which, of course, secretly you've always yearned for. So welcome, sweetheart, to…from here…to Eternity…

(EDRED's smile is mordant, but also infinitely sad.)

Slow fade on ELIZABETH's horror-stricken face as she strokes her blood-stained neck and realises what her destiny will be….)

THE END

LUCIFER'S FAIR

A HALLOWE'EN PLAY

Characters

HONOR
a white girl

THE POLICEMAN

CLIVE
a black boy

FANGS

WINNY

MISS BLYTON

SIR LUCIFER TOMBS

Lucifer's Fair was first performed at the Arts Theatre, Newport Street, London, WC2 on 30th October, 1976, with the following cast:

HONOR, Penny Casdagli
A POLICEMAN, Derek Fuke
CLIVE, Herbert Norville
FANGS, Nick Llewellyn
WINNY, Meryl Hampton
MISS BLYTON, Polly Taylor
SIR LUCIFER TOMBS, Clive Foster

Director, Nicholas Barter
Designer, Paul Dart
Music and Sound Effects, Ilona Sekacz
Lighting, Angus Stewart

PART ONE

SCENE ONE

The House Lights are still up. The CHILDREN and other members of the AUDIENCE are settling in their seats – when the entire Theatre is plunged into darkness! Moderate pandemonium.

Then we hear stereophonic, Satanic laughter. This is followed by the menacing voice of SIR LUCIFER TOMBS, who whispers; 'SIT DOWN AND LISTEN!' As his Satanic laughter dies away, we hear the opening music. Simultaneously the darkness is illuminated by huge fiery letters – which read 'TO LUCIFER'S FAIR'.

Time; the early 1970s.

In the distance we hear a GIRL singing.

All the songs are printed in the Berthold Baskerville Medium.

GIRL: **Let's all go to Lucifer's Fair,**
and win us the prize of a big brown bear,
and ride on the horse on the carousel,
and bang the hammer, and ring the bell,
for today there's winter in the air,
and today's the day of Lucifer's Fair.

(The LIGHTS come up and reveal the Gateway to 'Lucifer's Fair', over which there leans a sinister yew tree as…HONOR, an eleven year-old girl, enters repeating her song. Then she sings different words to the same melody.)

HONOR: **But when I go to Lucifer's Fair,**
I will challenge Lucifer when I'm there,
because of all the bad things he has done,
and I won't return until I've won,
so Sir Lucifer had best beware,
'cause today I'm coming to Lucifer's Fair.

(As HONOR finishes singing, there is a crash of thunder. Then a burly POLICEMAN cycles into view from the opposite direction. He brakes and confronts HONOR.)

POLICEMAN: Hey, you! Yeah, girl, I'm talkin' to you.

HONOR: Yes, Officer.

POLICEMAN: You seen a young lad round here? 'Bout your age?

HONOR: No.

POLICEMAN: 'Bout this tall. And runnin'.

HONOR: Away from you?

POLICEMAN: Yeah! He's bunked off from St Joseph's Orphanage, up behind Nightingale Wood. He's always runnin' away. An' I'm always havin' to chase him.

HONOR: Perhaps he doesn't like it there?

POLICEMAN: Sure he doesn't. But he's got no parents, so he'll have to go back to the orphanage, won't he? Now if you see him, you call the Police, right?

HONOR: Alright.

POLICEMAN: *(Going.)* His name's Clive Sobers. O.K.?

HONOR: O.K.

POLICEMAN: Hey! Why aren't *you* at school, anyway?

HONOR: Because it's Sunday, Officer.

POLICEMAN: Oh. So it is. But there's still no point in you hanging around here. The Fair's not open today. Or any other day. 'Fact in the week it's been here, I've never seen it open at all.

HONOR: I know.

POLICEMAN: Oh. *(Going.)* Well…afternoon.

HONOR: Afternoon, Officer.

(The POLICEMAN begins to cycle off, then breaks.)

POLICEMAN: Oh, the kid's got a football with him. Pinched it from St. Joseph's.

HONOR: Really?

POLICEMAN: Really. So if you see a football, you'll know the boot behind it belongs to Clive Sobers, right?

(The POLICEMAN laughs.)

HONOR: Right.

(The POLICEMAN cycles off.

The Opening Music begins again. HONOR gazes at the neon lettering over the Gateway to the Fair – as she sings.)

HONOR: **Let's all go to Lucifer's Fair,
and win us the prize of a big brown bear,
and ride on the horse on the carousel...**

(But HONOR is interrupted, and she jumps out of the way as a football bounces past her.)

CLIVE: *(Off.)* Jump for it, girl, jump for it!

(CLIVE, an eleven year-old boy, runs into view.)

CLIVE: Cor, you make a useless goalie! *(Expertly he retrieves the football.)* Anyway, you're supposed to dive and save it. Not hide from it, an' wave at it.

(CLIVE dribbles the ball around HONOR, showing off his footy skills. Then he demonstrates his heading expertise.)

HONOR: You must be...

CLIVE: *(Interrupting.)* Yeah. You runnin' away, too?

HONOR: No. Oh, don't worry. I won't turn you over to the cops – Clive Sobers.

CLIVE: How'd you know my name? Mind, it isn't really my name. 'Cause my parents left me as a baby in a cardboard box in this railway carriage 'cause they didn't want me. And I was found there by this train cleaner, who took me to St. Joseph's. Then this guy who runs St Joseph's, who's called Bradman, well, of course, 'e loves cricket; so 'e names me 'Clive', after Clive Lloyd, and 'Sobers', after Gary Sobers. *(HONOR looks perplexed.)* Yeah, I know; only the Wrinklies remember who those geezers were now! And, anyway, I 'ate cricket! So it's all been a waste of space, ent it? 'Cause footy's the only game for men. And I'm a genius at footy! *(But CLIVE's football-routine goes wrong.)* Most of the time. *(He kicks the ball to HONOR, who immediately starts to play basket ball with it as she dances circles around CLIVE.)* Hey, that's a stupid girls' game! Look, drop the ball, drop it an' kick it! *(She drops the ball.)* That's better. Now try and dribble it past me, and I'll show you how it's done.

(To CLIVE's amazement, HONOR not only dribbles the ball past him, but then she shoots it expertly into the wings.)

HONOR: A goal! A goal!

(Then HONOR runs around CLIVE like a triumphant professional footballer. CLIVE laughs, and gives her the obligatory footballer's hug, which she reciprocates. Then they break embarrassed.)

CLIVE: Wot did you say your name was?

HONOR: I didn't.

CLIVE: Oh.

HONOR: It's Honor. Honor Christabel Linthewaite.

CLIVE: Get a life.

HONOR: Whatever. But I'm going to the Fair. Are you coming?

(Before CLIVE can respond, there is the roar of an approaching motorbike.)

CLIVE: Oh hell, it's the Cops!

HONOR: Run, Clive, run!

FANGS: (*off/menacing.*) Stay where you are, both of you!

> *(The sound of the approaching motorbike becomes deafening as FANGS roars into view – on the POLICEMAN's bicycle. FANGS is dressed in the full Punk's gear, with static, rainbow-coloured hair. He is armed with knuckle-dusters and wears 'bovver' boots. The sound of the motorbike engine cuts out abruptly as FANGS jumps off the bicycle. FANGS laughs at the two gawking KIDS.)*

HONOR: Who are you?

FANGS: They call me – Fangs.

CLIVE: Where are they, then?

FANGS: Wot?

CLIVE: Yer fangs.

> *(FANGS produces a pair of plastic fangs.)*

FANGS: (*Sinister.*) 'Ere! I only put 'em in at night. See, if I 'ave 'em in all the time, I get mouth-ulcers. So, durin' the day, I use me fangs – to clean me nails.

> *(FANGS demonstrates.)*

HONOR: (*Pointing.*) That's that policeman's bike!

FANGS: (*Laughing.*) You bet ya! So if you both know what's good for you, you'll shove off, 'cause the Fair's closed.

CLIVE: Do *you* run the Fair, then? When you're not bitin' people.

FANGS: No, I'm only the Teeth around 'ere.

HONOR: Then who does run the Fair?

FANGS: My boss, Sir Lucifer Tombs.

HONOR: Then he's the man I've come to see. So now you can take me to see him.

FANGS: *(Laughing.)* You must be jokin', darlin'. 'E eats little sprogs like you for 'is supper.

HONOR: I still insist on seeing Sir Lucifer.

FANGS: *(Continuing to laugh.)* You 'insist'?

HONOR: Yes, because he is an evil, vile man, who is making my mother's life hell, so I intend to…

FANGS: *(Overriding her.)* You see this, Sweet Lips? *(FANGS brandishes his knuckle-duster.)* I made this in me metal-work classes. An' if you keep goin' on goin' on, you'll be chompin' on a knuckle-duster sarny!

HONOR: You don't frighten me, Fangs. What's more, when I meet your Boss, I'm going to tell him that he's an appalling landlord, who has no right to harass my poor Mum. And also I shall make it clear to Sir Lucifer that we have no intention of leaving our flat, so there's no point in him sending round his heavies anymore to ruin our plumbing and our electrics. Now be so good as to let me pass.

(CLIVE applauds HONOR's bravura.)

CLIVE: Fan-tas-tic! An I'll be your back-up, Honor.

FANGS: *(Brandishing his knuckle-duster.)* Right, darlin', you've arsked for it!

(FANGS grabs HONOR, but immediately CLIVE butts his head into FANG's midriff. Then they all collapse in a scrabbling heap.

At this moment, a middle-aged WOMAN wiggles into sight, dressed as Wonder Woman, complete with her golden tiara, Lasso of Truth and bullet-deflecting bracelets. But her Wonder Woman image is ruined because the middle-aged WOMAN is also carrying a battered suitcase, a plastic bag, plus she is wearing a long Manchester United scarf and an old pair of Wellies. Added to which, the WOMAN speaks

*with an American accent that leaves a lot to be desired – as she
confronts FANGS.)*

WONDER WOMAN: You take your hands off of the girl, or I'll
knock you from here to the land of the Amazons!

*(FANGS is so surprised by the arrival of WONDER WOMAN that,
momentarily, he is nonplussed.)*

FANGS: Who the 'ell are you, darlin'?

WONDER WOMAN: No one calls Wonder Woman 'darling'.
Now take me to Sir Lucifer before I duff you up good and
proper. *(Then from her plastic bag, WONDER WOMAN produces
a handful of letters that accidentally cascade onto the ground.)*
Because I've got enough incriminating evidence here to
transport you and the rest of Sir Lucifer's miserable gang to
the South Pole for the remainder of your lousy lives.

(HONOR helps WONDER WOMAN to pick up her letters.)

HONOR: Then you know that Sir Lucifer is a terrible crook.

WONDER WOMAN: You bet your sweet life, I do. *(FANGS
snatches the letters from them both.)* Hey, what d'you think
you're…?

(FANGS tears up the letters.)

FANGS: Where's your evidence now, baby?

WONDER WOMAN: Nobody calls Wonder Woman ' baby'!
(WONDER WOMAN whirls her Lasso of Truth around her head.)
And once I catch Lucifer in my Lasso of Truth, then he will
confess to the whole world the extent of his evil deeds.

FANGS: *(To WONDER WOMAN.)* Forget it , hun-bun, 'cause
you're gonna do nuffink! But I'm still gonna 'ave you
checked out, sugar lips, and if – as I suspect – you're all
mouth an' tights, then… *(He makes a throat-cutting gesture.)*
As for you kids, you'd best steer clear of Wonder Pooh
'ere… *(FANGS climbs on his bicycle.)* …or I'll 'ave your blood
bottled for my supper.

(As FANGS pedals off, we hear the roar of the disappearing motorbike. WONDER WOMAN grabs HONOR and CLIVE's hands.)

WONDER WOMAN: Now hold tight, you guys, and Wonder Woman will fly you to safety before you can say…

CLIVE: …Diana Prince?

WONDER WOMAN: Right!

HONOR: *(Breaking away.)* Sorry, Wonder Woman, but I'm going to the Fair.

CLIVE: So am I.

WONDER WOMAN: Now be sensible, you guys, and come with me before something terrible happens.

HONOR: Why should we trust you more than Fangs?

WONDER WOMAN: Because I'm Wonder Woman, and I can fly, so I can save you!

(But in her clumsy 'flying' demonstration, inadvertently WONDER WOMAN trips over her Manchester United scarf, and then over her battered suitcase, scattering all its contents. Then WONDER WOMAN lands flat on her face.)

CLIVE: It must be the Kryptonite.

(While HONOR is helping WONDER WOMAN to her feet, CLIVE is examining the spilt contents of her case, which proves to be a collection of costumes and disguises.)

WONDER WOMAN: Oh noodles and apfelstrudel!

(CLIVE pulls a Batman hood and cape out of the scattered contents of the suit case.)

CLIVE: You'd've been better to 'ave come here as Batman.

HONOR: Yes, because you're just not very good at disguising yourself, are you, Mrs…

MISS BLYTON: *(Now speaking in Upper Class English.)* Miss Enid Blyton, actually.

CLIVE: Oh not Noddy and Big Ears!

MISS BLYTON: What's wrong with Snotty and Fig Ears…I mean, of course, Dotty and Pig Ears… no, I mean…

HONOR: Yes, what *do* you mean, Miss Blyton?

MISS BLYTON: Heaven knows! But you must understand, I'm a Private Detective, so, most of the time, I'm a master of disguise. It's just occasionally I trip over myself, and then I drop things…and forget important bits of my costume and… *(As she re-packs her case.)* …yes, well, I suppose when you look at me closely, I have gone well past my sell-by date. But none of that's important now. No, the only thing that really matters is that you both get away from here pronto! --and leave *me* to deal with Lucifer.

(FANGS' voice echoes through the Theatre.)

FANGS: *(Off.)* BUT WOT CHANCE HAVE *YOU* GOT, BIG EARS? 'CAUSE THIS AINT TOYLAND, YOU NODDY!

(HONOR and CLIVE look round them nervously.)

MISS BLYTON: See what I mean? If you stay here, you both will be in the most terrible danger.

HONOR: We know.

CLIVE: But that's 'alf the fun of it all.

(Before MISS BLYTON can stop them, HONOR and CLIVE start to try on the disguises from her case.)

MISS BLYTON: Whatever do you think you're doing?

(HONOR puts on a false hooked nose and a witch's hat, while CLIVE picks up a topper and cane.

But as HONOR and CLIVE go into a song-and-dance routine, they fail to notice that FANGS is lurking in the shadows. Later FANGS joins in the singing.)

HONOR: **O I'm the Witch of the Midnight Sky.**

CLIVE: **And I'm the Duke of Edinburgh.**

(HONOR sings and points to MISS BLYTON.)

HONOR: **And she's a failed Private Eye.**

(FANGS sings to the AUDIENCE.)

FANGS: **And I'm the Fangs of Lucifer!**

HONOR/CLIVE: **Oh dear, oh lor!**
And we wonder what we've got in store.
Wo-ho! Wo-hey!
The world has gone mad today.
Yes, the world has gone mad today.

MISS BLYTON: *(Speaking.)* Oh do stop it, children, I beg you!

(HONOR and CLIVE ignore MISS BLYTON as they continue with their song-and-dance routine, with FANGS in tow.)

HONOR: **O I'm the Witch of the Midnight Sky.**

CLIVE: **And I'm the Duke of Edinburgh.**

HONOR: **And she's a failed Private Eye.**

FANGS: **And I'm the Fangs of Lucifer!**

HONOR/CLIVE: **Oh dear, oh lor!**
And we wonder what we've got in store.
Wo-ho! Wo-hey!
The world has gone mad today.
Yes, the world has gone mad today.

(They dance around MISS BLYTON, who hopelessly tries to stop them.)

MISS BLYTON: *(Speaking.)* We haven't time for a Song-and-Dance Number! You must go home. Your parents will be sick with worry. Teatime, you guys; you'll be late for your tea.

HONOR/CLIVE: *(Singing.)* **But we've no worries because we're free,**
and we're off to Lucifer's for tea.

(FANGS steps into a red spot and sings.)

FANGS: **For my Master's waiting in his lair.**
And once he gets you inside his Fair...

CLIVE: **...We'll turn Sir Lucifer into a stoat!**

HONOR: **Or perhaps into a nanny goat!**

MISS BLYTON: *(Speaking.)* No, children, he'll have you by the throat!

CLIVE: *(Singing.)* **No, she's the Witch of the Midnight Sky.**

HONOR: **And he's the Duke of Edinburgh.**

(In despair MISS BLYTON sings.)

MISS BLYTON: **Oh, and I'm the world's worst private Eye!**

FANGS: **And I'm the Fangs of Lucifer.**

(The FOUR of them sing the CHORUS.)

FOUR OF THEM: **Oh dear, oh lor!**
And we wonder what we've got in store.
Wo-ho! Wo-hey!
The world has gone mad today.
Yes, the world has gone mad today.
The world has gone mad today.

(The stage darkens, and FANGS turns on the other THREE as he sings.)

FANGS: *(Sinister, on echo.)* **Yes, the world has gone mad today.**

**And I tell you true; you'd better beware,
'cause no one comes home from Lucifer's fair!**

*(FANGS walks off into the darkness. The music fades away. The
CHILDREN stare after him, disconcerted by FANG's words.*

In the distance there is an ominous growl of thunder.)

MISS BLYTON: You see, even Fangs agrees with me, so it must
be true! Lucifer is just another name for the Devil. And
once you're in the Devil's power, he will utterly destroy
you.

HONOR: I still have to go to the Fair.

CLIVE: So do I.

MISS BLYTON: Why?

CLIVE: Someone's got to protect Honor – because, remember,
tonight is Hallowe'en.

MISS BLYTON: Exactly. That's why I've studied Lucifer's
methods, and all his crooked deals and his criminal set-up.
But they are nothing compared to what's in there! *(She
points to the illuminated sign over the Fair's Entrance.)* Once
you go inside Lucifer's Fair, you will find that nothing *is* as
it *seems.* Everyone – is someone else!

CLIVE: Wot?

MISS BLYTON: Yes, Clive. In there, you can't depend on
anyone. They are all dangerously unreliable.

HONOR: Adults generally are. That's nothing new.

CLIVE: And that, Miss Noddy, includes you.

MISS BLYTON: I beg your pardon?

HONOR: He's right, Miss B. Well, let's face it, you might be
one of Lucifer's hoods in disguise.

(In the distance we hear the Opening Theme.)

MISS BLYTON: Alright, if you don't believe me; on your own heads be it.

HONOR: *(Speaking.)* Well, Miss Big Ears…

(Singing.) **…We'd better be off to Lucifer's Fair.**

CLIVE: **And win us the prize of the big brown bear.**

HONOR/CLIVE: **And ride on the horse on the carousel, and bang the hammer and ring the bell; 'cause today it's Lucifer's turn to despair. When we break his spell over Lucifer's Fair!**

(Uneasily HONOR and CLIVE move off.

MISS BLYTON exits the other way, muttering.)

MISS BLYTON: I must find a telephone box that hasn't been vandalised! Before it's too late!

(Then we hear FANG's maniacal laughter stereophonically echo from the Fairground as…

….the LIGHTS FADE.)

SCENE TWO

LIGHTS come up to full to reveal a brightly-coloured Carousel, with flashing fairground lights – which has on it a skittle side-show, dominated by a shelf of prizes. In the midst of the prizes sits BRUNO, a life-size brown bear.

WINNY, an attractive, middle-class Witch, in a school gym slip, tennis shoes, cloak and witch's hat, steps off the Carousel. WINNY grins. Then she imitates the eerie call of a hunting owl.

In response to WINNY's call, FANGS appears.

WINNY: They're coming, Fangsy! I knew they would.

FANGS: You're really gonna enjoy this, Winny, ent you?

WINNY: I'm not a Gym-Slip-and-Hockey-Stick-Witch for nothing, sweetie.

FANGS: Has the Boss told you wot 'e wants the kids for?

WINNY: *(With a cackling laugh.)* The usual.

FANGS: Oh not annuver of them blood-thirsty experiments.

WINNY: You bet ya! Isn't it exciting? What are you doing?

(With the aid of a hand mirror, FANGS inserts his plastic fangs into his mouth.)

FANGS: I'm tryin' me new fangs out, ent I? *(Giving a vampire snarl.)* Wot you fink? D'you like 'em?

WINNY: They're spiffing. Makes you look like a right little raver.

FANGS: Yeah, an' they're just dyin' to sink into the succulent necks of them two kids.

WINNY: *(Gesticulating wildly.)* Quick, Fangs! Put your fangs away. The kids are coming!!

FANGS: *(Struggling with his fangs.)* 'Ang on, 'ang on! They've got jammed on me gums! OUCH!

WINNY: Now what have you done?

FANGS: I've bitten me blurry tongue! I should never've put me fangs in durin' daytime. They're lethal!

(WINNY helps FANGS to remove his fangs.)

WINNY: There! Your gnashers are out. Now, Fangs, put on the nearest thing you've got to a happy face, or those kids will think they've not come to a fairground, but to a graveyard.

FANGS: *(Pocketing his fangs and grinning horribly.)* How right they are!

(Simultaneously FANGS and WINNY turn Up-Stage for a moment. When they face the Audience again, we see they are wearing boaters and half-clown-masks, and they flourish Fred-Astaire dancing-canes.)

One! Two! Three!

(As HONOR and CLIVE enter…WINNY and FANGS go into their Welcoming-Song-and-Dance routine with their boaters and canes.)

FANGS: **Roll up, roll up!**
All the fun of the Fair.

WINNY: **Stroll up, stroll up!**
Win yourself a grizzly bear.

FANGS: **Roll up, roll up!**
See the Fair of the Year.

WINNY: **Stroll up, stroll up!**
There is nothing to fear.

FANGS/WINNY: **We've got hoop-la, skittles, too.**
Lots of things for you to do.

FANGS: **Our only wish is to please you.**

WINNY: *(Sinister.)* **Our only wish is to please…you.**

(WINNY cackles.)

FANGS: **Roll up, roll up!**
To Eternity.

WINNY: **Stroll up, stroll up!**
There's plenty to see.

FANGS: **Roll up, roll up!**
We do implore.

WINNY: **Stroll up, stroll up!**
There's room for more.

(HONOR and CLIVE watch in silence.)

FANGS/WINNY: **We've got puppets dressed in blue.**
Something old and something new.

FANGS: **Our only wish is to please you.**

WINNY: **Yes, our only wish is to please...** *(With a witch's laugh.)* **...you!**

FANGS/WINNY: **Try our lollies filled with goo; fizzy drinks by You Know Who!**

WINNY: **You Know Who!**

FANGS: **Roll up, roll up! All the fun of the Fair.**

WINNY: **Stroll up, stroll up! Win yourself a grizzly bear.**

FANGS: **Roll up, roll up! See the Fair of the Year.**

WINNY: **Stroll up, stroll up!**

FANGS: *(Speaking, very sinister.)* There is nothing to fear!

(WINNY and FANGS finish their dance routine with suitable boater-and-cane panache.

Then WINNY and FANGS doff their hats and masks, and they wait for the CHILDREN to applaud. But the CHILDREN only show their appreciation by slow-hand-clapping the PERFORMERS.)

HONOR: You're not bad. For adults. Not bad at all.

WINNY: Thank you, dear. And welcome to Lucifer's Fair.

HONOR: So where is Sir Lucifer, Miss er...?

WINNY: Not 'Miss'. Witch.

CLIVE: Which? Which what?

WINNY: Witch Winny.

HONOR: Which Winny? Who's Winny?

FANGS: She's Winny. I'm Fangs.

CLIVE: I'm Clive. She's Honor.

FANGS: He's Honor. She's Clive. I mean...

WINNY: I'm Fangs. He's Winny. I mean…

HONOR: So who's which?

WINNY: I'm which. I mean, I'm a witch, and he's a…

FANGS: *(Overriding her.)* Winny. Belt up! Now look, kids, if you want to come to our Fair, you've gotta prove you're bright enough to appreciate wot we've got on show here.

CLIVE: Bright enough?

WINNY: Yes, because no one enters Lucifer's Fair…

FANGS: …without first winning the Grizzly Bear!

(CLIVE points to BRUNO, the man-sized bear, who is sitting amidst the prizes on the Carousel.)

CLIVE: What you mean we gotta win that grotty, grizzly bear?

HONOR: Yes, and exactly what kind of Fair is this, anyway?

FANGS: It's a Fair of the Imagination.

WINNY: And of magic.

FANGS: Where nuffink is what it seems.

CLIVE: Honor, that's what Miss Crazy Big Ears said.

HONOR: Yes, and where's she disappeared to?

FANGS: I told you not to 'ave nuffink to do with her, didn't I?

WINNY: Because Miss Blyton is not what she seems, either.

HONOR: But there's no magic here, just skittles and that overgrown, moth-eaten bear.

(WINNY and FANGS begin their sinister singing incantation.)

WINNY: **The Supernatural only begins when Night comes.**

FANGS: **When the Blood-Sun sinks to the sound of… drums!**

(The stage darkens, and we hear a sinister, rhythmic accompaniment to FANGS' and WINNY's incantation, which grows and grows.)

WINNY: **And ghost-white mist crawls in from the sea...**

FANGS: **...and the Werewolf howls to the dead elm tree.**

WINNY: **Then everything's under Lucifer's Spell...**

FANGS: **...Insects and the animals...**

FANGS/WINNY: **...and Us as well!**

(Thunder and lightning as FANGS' and WINNY's incantation grows in power.)

FANGS: **Then Lucifer opens the Gates of Hell!**

WINNY: **And the Dead come forth to the Judgement Bell.**

FANGS: **The Vampire with his midnight sword...**

WINNY: **...bows low before the Great Dark Lord.**

FANGS: **The Wizard, Warlock and the Witch...**

WINNY: **...will come and make you children *rich!***

FANGS: **Tonight's the night!**
So if you're bright...

WINNY: **...we can arrange**
that you both change...

FANGS/WINNY: **...and have the same Power...**
...as *Us*, for One Hour!

(The music's tempo gets faster, and becomes more frenzied as FANGS and WINNY begin a macabre dance-routine around the now-spell-bound CHILDREN.)

FANGS/WINNY: **Then you can control the stars in the sky,**
and make it your wish, and you'll disappear.
Grow wings like a Dragon, and fly and fly.

WINNY: **Walk on the Moon, without any fear.**

FANGS: **Be Superman, and Wonder Woman...**

WINNY: **...and do everything that *they* can!**

FANGS: **Control the World as King and Queen!**

WINNY: **And make real for One Hour your Favourite Dream!**

(As the music continues, FANGS and WINNY speak above it..)

WINNY: It's the offer of a life-time!

FANGS: Don't dither on the brink.

WINNY: Sign on the dotted line!

FANGS: Well, wot d'you fink – of it so far?

CLIVE: *(Grinning.)* Rubbish!

WINNY: Oh.

HONOR: *(Singing.)* **But despite all that, you see, we're still coming to Lucifer's for tea.**

CLIVE: **So there's no need to be cross...**

HONOR: **...just because you lost the toss.**

(The CHILDREN go into their football-song-and-dance routine – while WINNY and FANGS sing a macabre counterpoint.)

CLIVE: **We're in a different league, you see.**

FANGS/WINNY: **Then Lucifer opens the Gates of Hell!**

HONOR: **We play for Arsenal, not Swansea.**

FANGS/WINNY: **And the Dead come forth to the Judgement Bell.**

CLIVE: **No one's as good at footy as me!**

FANGS/WINNY: **And the Vampire with his Midnight Sword.**

HONOR: **I float like a butterfly, and shoot like a bee!**

CLIVE: **But now, I'm afraid, we've reached the time…**

FANGS/WINNY: **The Wizard, Warlock and the Witch…**

HONOR: **…to end this stupid nursery rhyme.**

FANGS/WINNY: **…will come and make you children rich!**

CLIVE: **We're gonna win that grizzly bear…**

FANGS/WINNY: **…So tonight's the night!**

HONOR: **…and score a goal!**

CLIVE: **And score a goal!**

HONOR: **And score a goal!**

HONOR/CLIVE: **RIGHT INTO THE FAIR!!!!**

(HONOR kicks the football into the wings, and we hear the sound of falling skittles.)

WINNY: *(Speaking.)* Oh broomsticks and hemlock, what a magic shot!

CLIVE: Yeah, wicked, wicked, Honor! You've knocked down the lot!

(HONOR does the football war-dance of self-adulation. Then CLIVE gives her a fellow-professional hug.)

HONOR: So I'm the best, 'cause we've won, we've won!

CLIVE: Now we'll take the Prize Bear, an' then we'll be gone.

(The CHILDREN converge on BRUNO, but before they can reach him, BRUNO surges to his feet. BRUNO starts to cross the stage, when he is confronted by FANGS.)

FANGS: Hey, Bruno, you dumbo bear, where'd you fink you're orf to?

(With a ferocious growl BRUNO brushes FANGS aside.)

CLIVE: Bruno's gonna take us to Sir Lucifer, of course.

(BRUNO's growl becomes even more menacing.)

HONOR: Listen, he can growl like King Kong!

BRUNO: *(In a gruff, rumbling voice.)* And with a little encouragement, I can talk, too. But like Wicked Winny here and this disreputable Creature with the portable teeth, I am, also, not what I seem.

HONOR: If you're not a bear, what are you?

BRUNO: I'm a… I'm a…

(There is a sudden ear-piercing whistling sound that forces BRUNO to his knees, making him beat his head repeatedly on the ground. Obviously the BEAR is in the grip of one of SIR LUCIFER's most vicious Spells.)

BRUNO: *(Whimpering.)* No, Great Lucifer, have mercy on me, I beg you! I did not mean to defy you. I did not mean…

HONOR: Oh please don't upset yourself, Mr Bruno, please. We'll help you get free of that monster, Sir Lucifer. Won't we, Clive?

CLIVE: Dead right, we will!

FANGS: Oh no, you won't! *(FANGS inserts his plastic fangs into his mouth.)* 'Cause now it's Suppertime!

(FANGS moves in to bite CLIVE. Simultaneously WINNY snatches up her hockey-stick, and she advances on HONOR.)

WINNY: And this will learn you, my gel, for answering Teacher back! Ready, Fangsy? One!

FANGS: Two!

WINNY: Three!

(At that moment MISS BLYTON, dressed in her Hell's Angel red-leather gear, complete with crash helmet, bounces onto the Stage on…a skate board! MISS BLYTON challenges WINNY and FANGS.)

MISS BLYTON: OK, if you two snakes wanna rumble… *(MISS BLYTON falls off her skateboard.)* …I'll give you both a rumble that you'll never forget! *(She lands flat on her face.)* OWWW! *(FANGS and WINNY laugh. They stop menacing the CHILDREN, and instead they advance on MISS BLYTON.)* Oh dear, I've laddered my leather!

(FANGS and WINNY haul MISS BLYTON to her feet.)

FANGS: Wot perfect timing, Miss Big Ears! You're gonna be the ideal replacement for Bruno.

WINNY: As our Super-Duper De Luxe Prize!

(As WINNY and FANGS push MISS BLYTON towards the Carousel, there is the sudden, amplified crack of a whip!

Everyone freezes.

SIR LUCIFER TOMBS appears, complete with waxed moustaches, goatee beard, grey topper, red waistcoat, tails and a large black cloak with a fur collar. He has a clubfoot and walks with a pronounced limp. SIR LUCIFER carries a ringmaster's whip.)

SIR LUCIFER: *(exuding the full silken charm.)* Ah my dear children, sweet Miss Blyton, a very good afternoon to you all.

HONOR: Are you…?

SIR LUCIFER: Indeed I am, Pretty Miss Honor. Sir Lucifer Tombs, at your service. And may I say how delighted I am, to welcome you all to my…

CLIVE: *(Interrupting.)* Look, cut all that smarmy talk, and…

HONOR: …Defend yourself against the following charges!

FANGS: Hey, kids! Don't you realise you're addressin' a Great…

HONOR: …Big, cowardly, nasty, horrible…

FANGS: …Bullyin', rotten, filthy, crooked…

HONOR: …Monster! – who's made my mother's life so miserable!

CLIVE: Well, it's true, Sir Lucifer. Your thugs've messed up 'er Mum's plumbin' and…

HONOR: …As a result, our ground floor was flooded, and everything was ruined.

FANGS: Also they screwed up 'er Mum's wirin'…

HONOR: …So she almost electrocuted herself!

FANGS: An' then they made 'er gas-stove 'ave a terrible explosion…

HONOR: …And we still haven't got all the apple pie and lamb stew off the ceiling!

MISS BLYTON: And that's only one poor family, Sir Lucifer, that you have been a vile landlord to. The story is the same with all the houses you own. Most of them have rising damp, faulty power-connections, doors that jam, mouldy walls and rotting floorboards – and that's just in the basements.

SIR LUCIFER: *(Smiling beneficently.)* Oh come, come, come, come, my dears. There is a slight misunderstanding here. But have no fear, I will have all your little complaints looked into. *(Hissing SIR LUCIFER advances on WINNY and FANGS.)* And if I discover that any of my craven minions have dared to harass even one of my esteemed tenants, I assure you that the minion in question will spit slowly over a very hot roast… What I mean, of course, is roast slowly over a very hot spit. This I swear as a gentleman and a… Yes, well, never mind. But to prove I am a man of my word and a 'devil' of a fellow – here! And here! And here! *(To the CHILDREN's amazement, SIR LUCIFER conjures dozens of five pound notes out of the air. As the notes are fluttering to the ground, the CHILDREN snatch them out of the air and shove them in their pockets.)* Yes, you don't need to be afraid to pocket them, my dears; they're all for you! And there are plenty more five pound notes where they come from. Indeed, I am only too pleased to give you all the money you need, Honor, to help your distraught mother. And I will bestow even more on you, Clive, so you can buy yourself some proper parents. And there's even some for you, Miss Blyton, so you can purchase your very own detective agency. But you can only have the rest of the money, my dears;

if...you come to my Fair tonight,

when the Hallowe'en moon shines bright.

(SIR LUCIFER conjures a few more five-pound notes out of the air, followed by – if possible – a stuffed raven!.) Oh, stuff a pumpkin! That was supposed to be a white dove. But, unfortunately, I only ever seem to produce ravens. I wonder why...

HONOR: *(Counting the five-pound notes.)* I've never seen so much money, Clive, have you?

CLIVE: No, it's like winnin' the Lottery! An' just fink wot we can do wiv it?

MISS BLYTON: Don't touch those notes, children! Throw them back at him. They're all bound to be forged or stolen!

(SIR LUCIFER pats the CHILDREN's heads affectionately.)

SIR LUCIFER: So, my dears, you will come to my Hallowe'en Party, then.

HONOR: Well...

SIR LUCIFER: Excellent, Honor. I thought you might.

MISS BLYTON: No, no, the very last thing you must do is spend Hallowe'en here!

HONOR: There's more money, you say.

CLIVE: Yeah, are you really gonna give us even more money?

SIR LUCIFER: Yes, lots and lots more. 'Fact I can give you anything you like. Everything! *(Smiling.)* At a price.

MISS BLYTON: But at what price?

SIR LUCIFER: Oh, and I almost forgot, my dears. Here are your presents for my Hallowe'en Party. *(He conjures colourfully-wrapped presents from under his voluminous black cloak.)* That's yours, Honor. And here's yours, Clive. And last, but never least, this is yours, Miss Blyton. No, no, no, my dears! It's better you don't open then until tonight.

(The LIGHTS dim.

Music. FANGS and WINNY start a sinuous dance around the CHILDREN and MISS BLYTON. It is like the Dance of Death as SIR LUCIFER sings.)

SIR LUCIFER: **O come tonight
to Lucifer's Fair,
when the moon shines bright
on the children's hair.
And meet my friends,
and face your fate,
where the Rainbow ends.
So don't be late!**

(FANGS and WINNY dance around the partially-spellbound CHILDREN and MISS BLYTON as LUCIFER sings.)

**And have no fear
at Lucifer's Fair.
It's the Night of the Year
to do what you dare.
It's Hallowe'en Night,
when the world is in gloom,
and the moon shines bright;
so we'll see you soon.**

(SIR LUCIFER laughs. FANGS and WINNY continue their sinister dance routine around the entranced CHILDREN.)

SIR LUCIFER: **O come tonight
to Lucifer's Fair,
when the moon shines bright**

> **on the children's hair.**
> **And meet my friends,**
> **and face your fate,**
> **where the Rainbow ends.**
> **So don't be late!**

(SIR LUCIFER gives a sepulchral laugh.)

MISS BLYTON: *(Speaking.)* You mustn't go, children, You mustn't go! Promise me you won't go!

HONOR/CLIVE: *(Singing in a trance.)*
> **We'll come tonight**
> **to Lucifer's Fair.**
> **It's the Night of the Year**
> **to do what we dare.**
> **It's Hallowe'en Night,**
> **when the world is in gloom,**
> **and the moon shines bright.**
> **So we'll see you soon.**
> **Under the light of the silvery moon.**

MISS BLYTON: *(speaking.)* You can't go, you can't!

(SIR LUCIFER swirls his cloak and disappears – in a puff of smoke! MISS BLYTON and the CHILDREN are left stunned – while FANGS and WINNY dance off to the haunting Opening Melody.

Slow fade to BLACKOUT.)

SCENE THREE

Same setting as Scene One. The Gateway to Lucifer's Fair.

It is twilight, with the sound of crickets and birdsong.

HONOR and CLIVE come into view, carrying plastic carrier bags. Instantly they are confronted by BRUNO the Bear, who is dancing clumsily to the melody of a street-organ.

HONOR: I wish I knew whether we could trust Miss Blyton.

CLIVE: I don't fink we should. Well, she's gone an' disappeared again, ent she? *(He passes HONOR an apple from his bag.)* 'Ere, this is the last apple we got.

HONOR: Mm…they're absolutely scrumptious.

CLIVE: Yeah, though I say so meself, I am a scrumpin' genius. *(To the dancing BRUNO.)* You 'ungry, Bruno?

BRUNO: No, I'm too brimful of misery.

HONOR: Please sit down, Mr Bruno. Well, it must be so exhausting dancing like that for hours on end.

BRUNO: It is – but dancing's the only thing that stops me thinking.

CLIVE: Finkin' wot?

BRUNO: Thinking of what I used to be before Sir Lucifer put his spell on me.

HONOR: *(Laughing.)* Oh come now, Mr Bruno, Sir Lucifer never put a spell on anyone. He's just a cheap conjuror.

BRUNO: You couldn't be more wrong!

(Off, the melody of the street-organ stops abruptly. HONOR waves several five-pound notes at CLIVE.)

HONOR: So what are you going to spend yours on, then?

CLIVE: Nuthin'.

HONOR: What d'you mean?

CLIVE: I bet they're forged.

HONOR: They aren't!

CLIVE: Are!

HONOR: Aren't!

CLIVE: Are!

HONOR: Aren't!

CLIVE: You don't know wot you're talkin' about. You ent got a clue!

HONOR: Oh yes, I have. I'm not an ignorant, little orphan.

CLIVE: No, you're just a snotty-nosed, stuck-up dobber! *(Going.)* So I'm off 'ome!

HONOR: You haven't got a home.

CLIVE: Right then, you go to Lucifer's 'Allowe'en party by yerself – and I 'ope you scare yourself to death!

HONOR: *(Suddenly nervous.)* Nothing scares me! *(Stuttering.)* N-n-nothing…

CLIVE: Then, best of luck, Snob-chops.

(BRUNO intervenes.)

BRUNO: Now stop it, stop it! Both of you, stop all that!

HONOR: Stop all what?

BRUNO: Stop letting Sir Lucifer control you.

CLIVE: 'E ent controllin' us.

BRUNO: That's where you are both so wrong. Without you realising it, Sir Lucifer is deliberately making you fight with each other. It's all part of his demonic plan to destroy you both. As *I* know to my cost. *(SIR LUCIFER's maniacal laughter echoes throughout the Theatre.)* You see, until this morning, I wasn't a great lumbering bear, I was...I was...

(SIR LUCIFER's Satanic laughter increases.)

HONOR: You were what, Mr Bruno? You can tell us.

(With his paws over his ears, BRUNO tries to shut out LUCIFER's laughter which continues to increase.)

BRUNO: I was...I was a... *(Now SIR LUCIFER's laughter is so deafening, it forces BRUNO to slump to his knees.)* Stop it, Master, stop it! Please, I beg you! *(But SIR LUCIFER's laughter is relentless – and the CHILDREN are terrified.)* I... was...a...

(BRUNO slumps unconscious to the ground. Then LUCIFER's ear-splitting laughter stops abruptly.)

CLIVE: What the hell was that?

HONOR: I don't know, but Sir Lucifer thought it was funny. And look what it's done to Bruno! So perhaps he is telling us the truth.

CLIVE: 'Bout Sir Lucifer?

HONOR: About everything! Well, what if Bruno *isn't* Bruno, but he's some poor soul that's been changed by Sir Lucifer into a bear? And what if Lucifer is planning...?

CLIVE: ...To do the same to us?

HONOR: Right.

CLIVE: *(Pulling a present out of his carrier bag.)* So are we gonna open these presents he gave us, or not?

HONOR: D'you think we should?

CLIVE: Well, it's better than us just standin' around 'ere scarin' ourselves stupid, ent it?

HONOR: Yes. Then...here goes. *(They both unwrap their parcels to reveal – a Witch's and Wizard's costume respectively.)* Stroll on. *(Laughing.)* D'you think we're supposed to wear these at the Party?

CLIVE: Wot else can we do wiv 'em?

(As the CHILDREN start to clamber into their 'magical' costumes, BRUNO stirs. When BRUNO realises what they are doing, he shakes his head vehemently.)

HONOR: Clive, look! Mr Bruno's trying to tell us something.

CLIVE: No way.

HONOR: I wish Miss Blyton was here, so we could…well, discuss things.

(At that moment two broomsticks, thrown by unseen hands from either side of the stage, clatter at the CHILDREN's feet, making them jump.)

CLIVE: 'Ell's bells! Bloomin' broomsticks!

HONOR: Another of Sir Lucifer's nasty spells.

CLIVE: *(Picking up a broomstick.)* Yeah, but I could no more fly orf on this than…

HONOR: …Mr Bruno can talk? *(As the stage darkens.)* And, look, it's gone suddenly very dark now, hasn't it? So even if we wanted to go to Sir Lucifer's Hallowe'en Party, we couldn't possibly see our way. *(Eerie music steals through the growing night. Then the Gate to the Fair swings open to reveal – several lighted pumpkins in the skittles' gallery.)* Oh dear! How very thoughtful of…someone.

(An owl hoots. HONOR shrieks.)

CLIVE: Don't be scared, Honor. 'S'just an old barn owl. *(Nervous.)* I 'ope.

HONOR: Of course it's only an owl.

(Off, there is a frightening, stereophonic WITCH's cackle.)

CLIVE: *(Gasping.)* Oh strewth!

HONOR: What's the matter, Clive? It was only a mad witch cackling over the heath.

CLIVE: That's why my hair's standin' on end.

HONOR: Really? It doesn't show.

(The owl hoots again, and, off, the WITCH laughs maniacally which make the CHILDREN jump.)

HONOR: *(Her teeth chattering.)* Can you see where those candles are…exactly?

CLIVE: Yeah…they seem to be among them…tombstones.

HONOR: Tombstones?

CLIVE: Yeah. I fink this Fair 'as been set up among all these… *(Stuttering.)*…t-t-tombstones.

HONOR: But don't you think it's a little odd that Sir Lucifer is giving His Hallowe'en Party in a g-graveyard?

CLIVE: Oh I dunno. Dracula often 'as 'is meals in a graveyard.

HONOR: Quite. So perhaps it will help if we sing a little ditty.

CLIVE: Right. One.

HONOR: Two.

CLIVE: Th-three!

    (Singing.) **When the twilight falls,
and the sky goes black…**

HONOR: **…When the Screech Owl calls,
and we're on the rack…**

TOGETHER: **…Then it's time, then it's time, then it's
time…**

    (Looking nervously at each other.) **…TO GO BACK!**

HONOR: **When the Werewolf howls,
and the graveyard's dark…**

CLIVE: **...When the Vampire prowls,
and the Banshees bark...**

TOGETHER: **...Then run fast, then run fast, then run
fast...**

(Looking nervously at one another.) **...TO THE PARK!**

CLIVE: **When the Grey Witch flies,
and the White Ghosts moan...**

HONOR: **...When our courage dies,
and we are alone...**

TOGETHER: **...Then it's time, then it's time, then it's
time...**

(looking nervously at one another.) **...TO RUN HOME!**

*(The CHILDREN are about to retreat when MISS BLYTON, in her
witch's gear, plus broomstick, swings into view on a rope! – and
collides with the CHILDREN. They all land in a heap.)*

CLIVE: *(Speaking.)* Who'd you fink you are? Our Fairy
Godmother?

MISS BLYTON: *(Doing her best Witch's voice.)* No, my pretties;
I'm the kind old Witch of Bloomsbury Common.

HONOR: Oh, Miss Blyton, you're hopeless. You're utterly
hopeless.

MISS BLYTON: You mean, you can see through my disguise?

CLIVE: Yup.

MISS BLYTON: And I didn't scare you.

HONOR: Nope.

MISS BLYTON: Oh scorpions and dung beetles! What a dismal
failure I am. Even my witch's hat's got a dent. And every
blasted telephone box in a radius of two miles is bust.
(Registering their costumes.) Hey, why ever are you two
dressed up like that?

HONOR: Because we're going to liven up Sir Lucifer's Hallowe'en Party, of course. Right, Clive?

CLIVE: Right.

MISS BLYTON: You can't go into that Fair, either of you. It's too dangerous.

HONOR: We have to go, because it's our only chance to collect more money from Sir Lucifer to help my mother.

MISS BLYTON: That's nothing but a ruse to lure you into his Satanic web!

HONOR: And if he doesn't give us the money he promised us, we'll get the proof that he's a dangerous crook, and then we'll go to the Police and have him arrested. *(To CLIVE.)* So what are you waiting for? Let's go.

MISS BLYTON: You can't go! And, anyway, you'll prove nothing because Sir Lucifer is not what he seems. Nor is Winny, or Fangs. None of them are. And that also includes Bruno!

(The CHILDREN stare at the motionless BRUNO.)

CLIVE: Surely Bruno's not unreliable?

MISS BLYTON: Oh yes, he is! *(There is a sudden ear-piercing whistle from the graveyard, followed by a staccato drum-beat. In response, BRUNO, like an automaton, drags himself to his feet. Then the BEAR is pulled off stage, as if by an unseen force – in the direction of the graveyard.)* You see, my dears, Mr Bruno is *very* unreliable.

HONOR: Yes, I see…

CLIVE: Sorry, but if Bruno can go to a Hallowe'en Party in a graveyard, so can I. *(There is a crash of thunder that makes CLIVE jump.)* Oh, 'Ell!

(A searing flash of lightning illuminates a MIDNIGHT HAG, who flies into view – or materialises above the Fair Gateway. Her presence is terrifyingly malevolent.)

HAG: *(Cackling.)* Welcome, to Lucifer's Realm – humans! *(In the now-menacing darkness, the HAG seems to glow above the CHILDREN, as she is suffused in ultra-violet light. An unearthly cackle of malefic laughter echoes through the night, backed by more lighting and thunder.)* Do not try to speak, humans – YOU ARE DUMB! And you are now the Servants of Lucifer, and as such you are privileged to watch all the Creatures of Hell as they scream through the whistling air to do my Master's Bidding on this Hallowe'en, because this is the night when Lucifer will enslave the World!

(The thunder explodes into the HAG's Song.)

HAG'S SONG: **Tonight is the night when the Dead awake;**
when the Spirits and Goblins and Cats;
when the Lizards and Toads and Blood-sucking Bats
take over the Earth, and bite, and break
the hearts of the Children,
hearts of the Children,
hearts of the Children – who lie awake!

(The HAG gives a chilling screech of laughter. MISS BLYTON and the CHILDREN are now transfixed with fear.)

HAG'S SONG: **Hallowe'en, my dears, is the Night of the**
year,
when the Dark is filled with Horror and Fear!
So, wherever you are; Beware! Beware!
The Dead are coming! Despair! Despair!
Of your Minds, your Souls; take care, take care!
You've arrived – at Lucifer's Fair!

(The HAG cackles like a demented witch. Then the next moment she lets out what can only be described as 'a girlish giggle', as she throws back her cloak, removes her witch's hat and mask to reveal – the delectable WINNY.)

MISS BLYTON: Oh my sainted aunt – it's only you, Winny.

HONOR: Yes, for a moment we thought…

WINNY: *(Still laughing.)* …That I was an evil old hag? I know. I just couldn't resist it. You see, I love scaring the pants off people.

MISS BLYTON: It was unforgivable, Winny!

CLIVE: Yeah, you really got us goin'!

WINNY: *(Thrilled.)* Did I really? How absolutely spiffing. But let me tell you; my hockeystick performance is nothing compared to what we have in store for you – in the graveyard.

(WINNY gives another blood-curdling, witch-like cackle. Immediately she is answered by FANGS' equally-demonic laughter from inside the graveyard. Then a sinister pipe and drum echo through the night as the stage darkens ominously.)

MISS BLYTON: *(Disconcerted.)* What are you doing now, Winny?

HONOR: Why have you got that strange look in your eyes, Winny?

CLIVE: Yes, why are you smilin' like that, Winny?

(WINNY beckons menacingly.)

WINNY: Welcome…to Lucifer's Fair…*mortals.*

(The CHILDREN move forward as if in a trance.)

MISS BLYTON: Children, I beg you, please don't go into the Fair!

CLIVE: *(Taking HONOR's hand.)* We must.

MISS BLYTON: But, children…

HONOR: Where ever there is Evil, Miss B…

CLIVE: …It's got to be destroyed!

(Ghostly, hypnotic music envelops the CHILDREN as the mist begins to roll in from the graveyard.)

WINNY: You are right, my dears; come to the Fair. Now look behind you; the blind worms are following, the grass snakes, leather jackets, wasps, hornets, dung flies and spotted spiders. They are all moving through the autumn leaves…into the freezing mist…as they must…as they come to pay their homage to the Dark Lord, and bow their heads before Great Lucifer's Throne.

(Now in a trance, the CHILDREN wave to the frozen figure of MISS BLYTON. Then the CHILDREN go off singing.)

HONOR/CLIVE: **O we are going to Lucifer's Fair,**
to over-turn great Lucifer's Throne;
to bring the singing birds back in the air,
and turn his evil face to stone,
because we believe the World is green;

HONOR: **And CLIVE shall be King!**

CLIVE: **And HONOR be Queen!**

(The CHILDREN are swallowed up in the mist. MISS BLYTON is about to follow them.)

WINNY: *(Imperiously raising her arm.)* Woman, you cannot enter here! Return from whence you came!

(The now-seemingly bewitched MISS BLYTON is compelled to exit the other way.

WINNY cackles with laughter. There is a blinding flash of lightning, and WINNY flies out – or disappears – in the darkness that follows.

There is a crash of thunder. The Carousel turns to reveal… BRUNO, standing with his back to us.

Another flash of lightning.

BRUNO turns, and we see he is wearing the head of… KING KONG! His baleful eyes stare at the Audience. He is wielding a gigantic, spiked club.

Thunder. Lightning.

BRUNO beats his chest and lets out a blood-curdling roar. The roar is taken up by the horns and percussion – as BRUNO advances with his raised club on the now-cowering CHILDREN in the Front Row of the Stalls.

He is about to bring his club down on the AUDIENCE's heads when – there is a sudden BLACKOUT! And an INTERVAL.)

END OF PART ONE

PART TWO

SCENE ONE

Five minutes before Curtain Up, HONOR and CLIVE (still in their Witch's and Wizard's gear respectively) join the ice-cream queue in the Auditorium with the other CHILDREN.

As they eat their ice-creams, HONOR and CLIVE chat with the members of the AUDIENCE.

There is a deafening peal of thunder – and the LIGHTS black out in the Auditorium. HONOR and CLIVE exit unseen in the darkness.

The Curtain rises – and we see the Fair's Carousel is set in the sinister Graveyard.

It is now full night, and grotesque Hallowe'en pumpkins glimmer in between the forbidding gravestones. An eerie wind keens around the tombs like a spirit in torment.

Then there is a prolonged scream. It sounds like HONOR. But her scream is silenced by the WITCH's triumphant cackle.

Silence.

The CHILDREN, both looking very scared, steal into view. They are still in their Witch's and Wizard's gear respectively. HONOR carries a broomstick while CLIVE has a Gandalf-like Wizard's staff.

CLIVE: Stroll on!

HONOR: Yes, it is very spooky, isn't it?

CLIVE: Wot a place to 'ave an 'Allowe'en Party!

>   *(The WITCH cackles again – only this time from the opposite direction, but now the WITCH is much nearer. The CHILDREN spin around.)*

HONOR: *(Calling off.)* Miss Blyton? Is that you playing games, Miss B?

CLIVE: No, she's gone an' done a runner. Typical woman.

HONOR: I beg your pardon?

CLIVE: Oh don't get your knickers in a twist, Hon. I don't count you as a woman.

HONOR: I'm relieved to hear it. So what do we do now?

CLIVE: Good question.

HONOR: All these tombs are giving me goose pimples all over.

CLIVE: Look what they're doin' to my Affro-cut.

HONOR: *(Calling off.)* Sir Lucifer! So where's the money you promised us?

CLIVE: Yeah, bring out all your dosh, an' come an' show yerself.

HONOR: *(Rhyming with him.)*
'Cause we've come to your Fair for our share of your wealth.

CLIVE: It's true, Sir Lucifer, we are really 'ere…

HONOR: …Looking quite stupid in our witches' gear.

CLIVE: You said we'd have a real Hallowe'en Party…

HONOR: …So bring on the food, and let's get hearty!

CLIVE: Lots of ice cream an' chocolate cake…

HONOR: …To give us the trots and the stomach-ache!

(The CHILDREN laugh, and then invitingly sing to the Audience.)

HONOR: **We invite you all to laugh and joke.**
We've got tons of sweets and Diet Coke.
It's the perfect place, you must agree;

CLIVE: **…with a yawning tomb…**

HONOR: **…and a corpse or three!**

TOGETHER: **Ha-ha-ha! Let's have a party!
Come on in!**

CLIVE: **Welcome, my friends; everything's free.**

HONOR: **Come to our disco and dance with me.**

CLIVE: **Reggie with a reptile, go snogging with a snake.**

HONOR: **Boogie with a bogey, to make the Dead awake!**

TOGETHER: **Ha-ha-ha! Let's have a party!**

CLIVE: **Come on in!**

(They go into a Dance Routine.)

HONOR: **The graveyard is hopping. It's all systems go.**

CLIVE: **We want some action. Get on with the Show.**

HONOR: **A turn on the thumbscrews, a stretch on the
rack.**

CLIVE: **Take a ride on the Ghost Train that never comes
back.**

TOGETHER: **Ha-ha-ha! Let's have a party!
Come on in!**

CLIVE: **Here's your invitation.**

HONOR: **The Witching Hour is come.**

CLIVE: **The blood is bubbling nicely,**

HONOR: **And the tongue is overdone.**

CLIVE: **Fangs is grilling punk steaks while Winny's frying
flies,**

HONOR: **While Lucifer is making jellies out of eyes!**

TOGETHER: **Ha-ha-ha! Let's have a party!
Yes, let's...have...a...Party. COME ON IN!**

CLIVE: *(Speaking.)* Stroll on! If we go on like this, we'll end up as nutty as Witch Winny.

HONOR: *(Moving away.)* Yes, perhaps we should just go home. My Mum's sure to be very worried about where I am by now.

CLIVE: 'S'alright for you. I aint got no 'ome to go to.

HONOR: Yes, but we can't just…well, go on wandering around here, scaring ourselves to death.

CLIVE: That's part of the test, ent it?

HONOR: What is?

CLIVE: The waitin' around for somefink to 'appen. There's always a scene like this in the movies. You know, when the hero, whether it's Doctor Who, or Batman,, well, they 'ave to…just stand around an' wait until the Bad Guys suddenly jump on 'em! *(Without warning, CLIVE grabs HONOR's neck. She screams.)* Sorry, Hon. But I 'ad to try it.

HONOR: That's OK. I wasn't really scared. Just don't do it again.

(Sinister drums start to beat in the distance.)

CLIVE: Shush! Listen! Somefink's about to 'appen! I can feel it…can't you?

HONOR: Yes…

CLIVE: We'd better make a plan quick.

HONOR: What kind of plan?

CLIVE: Any kind. *(Pointing to a tombstone.)* Well, you see wot's on this tombstone?

HONOR: *(Reading the inscription on the tombstone.)* 'Here lies the mortal remains of…Sir Lucifer Tombs.'

CLIVE: But we were only talkin' to Sir Lucifer this… afternoon…

HONOR: Yes, and then he seemed…very much alive!

(The CHILDREN are so engrossed at looking at SIR LUCIFER's tomb, they fail to notice TWO HOODED FIGURES, who have appeared in the night mist. The HOODED FIGURES are carrying a shining black coffin.

The CHILDREN gasp as they become aware of the INTRUDERS.

The HOODED FIGURES ignore the CHILDREN, and they place the coffin in the middle of the graveyard, accompanied by the desolate sound of a tolling funeral bell. CLIVE goes up to one of the HOODED FIGURES.)

CLIVE: Hey, mister…who's in that coffin?

(The HOODED FIGURES turn on CLIVE, and we see that they have no faces – only hollow skulls! Then the HOODED FIGURES glide off into the night mist as the wind keens over the dead leaves.)

HONOR: The waiters at this Hallowe'en Party are toffee-nosed plonkers, aren't they?

CLIVE: Shush!

(CLIVE beckons to HONOR, who joins him by the coffin. The sound of the wind increases.)

HONOR: Suddenly it's gone…very cold…hasn't it?

CLIVE: Yup.

HONOR: And the moon's disappeared.

CLIVE: Yup.

HONOR: *(Pointing fearfully.)* Oh no! What are those…things, flitting between the branches?

CLIVE: Bats. There are just 'undreds an' thousands of b-b-bats with big teeth!

HONOR: Look! The lid of the coffin is…moving!

CLIVE: Wot a way to start a party! *(As the coffin lid continues to open slowly, mist oozes out of the coffin, followed by…)* Ent that a…hand comin' out of the coffin?

HONOR: No. It's just a silly old…c-c-claw!

CLIVE: Wot ever it is; it needs its nails cuttin'!

(The coffin lid crashes to the ground, and a black claw, followed by a black-swathed arm, reaches out towards the cowering CHILDREN!.)

HONOR: Perhaps we should give it…a helping hand.

CLIVE: Don't you mean…'claw'? And it's getting' colder an' colder.

(From inside the coffin, there is a prolonged, chilling hiss.)

HONOR: It sounds as if *he's* a touch chilly, too!

(Then FANGS, who is dressed like Count Dracula, slowly levers himself to his feet from within the coffin. His bat's cape is spread out in traditional vampire style. Simultaneously there is a searing flash of lightning, followed by a deafening clap of thunder. FANGS responds by going into his snarling, eye-bulging and fangs-flashing vampire routine.)

FANGS: What lovely, white, succulent throats you both have! *(FANGS lunges towards the CHILDREN, but in his eagerness, he trips over the side of the coffin, and lands flat on his face.)* OWWWW!!!

HONOR: Oh, what a shame. Dracula's spoilt his first entrance.

FANGS: *(Awkwardly clambering to his feet.)* Blast these bloomin' bovver-boots! They're more trouble than their worth. Mind, they're alright durin' the day for puttin' the boot in, but at night they certainly get in the way of the bitin'.

(Snarling and hissing, FANGS advances on HONOR and CLIVE.)

CLIVE: Oh Fangs, get real. You aint Count Dracula. You aint got big enough teeth.

FANGS: Wot you mean, I aint got big enough teeth? *(He feels inside his mouth – and he discovers he has forgotten to put his fangs in!.)* Oh spit and saliva! I knew somefink was missin'! I'd forget my bat's wings if they weren't pinned on. (*He pulls his plastic fangs out of his pocket.)* This is wot 'appens when you got false teeth. *(He puts his fangs into his mouth and snarls.)* Ahhhh! All this messin' about has given me the most terrific thirst!

(FANGS lunges towards them again, making the appropriate vampire noises. HONOR laughs.)

HONOR: I'm sorry, Fangsy, but you're just pathetic.

FANGS: *(Pulling himself up short.)* Eh? Why?

HONOR: Well, you shouldn't be stumbling around like Coco the Clown.

FANGS: *(Suddenly pathetic.)* Wot should I be doin', then?

HONOR: For a start, you should give those great black wings of yours a big flap. Then you should take off – and swoop down on us like Dracula does!

CLIVE: *(To FANGS.)* Well, don't just stand there like a wally. Get flappin'.

(FANGS flaps his wings frenetically.)

HONOR: Not bad. Now fly off!

FANGS: I can't. I forgot me jet-pack. Look, d'you mind if I stop all this flippin' flappin'? 'Cause it's getting' all bloomin' breezy around me bum!

CLIVE: Who's ever 'eard of a vampire who can't fly?

FANGS: *(Snarling.)* I can bite, though. I can bite!

(FANGS charges at them, but again he trips over the coffin. Cursing FANGS pulls himself to his feet when MISS BLYTON, now dressed as Florence Nightingale, appears with her lamp.)

MISS BLYTON: Enough of that Dracula nonsense, sirrah!

HONOR: Oh, Miss Blyton.

MISS BLYTON: I am not Miss Blyton. *(Waving her lamp.)* As you can see, because of my famous lamp, I am Florence Nightingale come to rescue you both.

CLIVE: Florrie Nightingale didn't get mixed up with vampires, did she?

MISS BLYTON: No, more's the pity.

FANGS: Stop it, all of you, stop it! How can you joke an' giggle when Fangs, the Vampire Bat, is on the rampage for children's blood?

(FANGS charges at the CHILDREN, but MISS BLYTON holds him at bay with her lamp. Simultaneously she hides HONOR and CLIVE behind her nurse's cloak. Then she passes them both something.)

MISS BLYTON: Here, chew this, chew this!

HONOR: What is it, Miss B?

MISS BLYTON: Just eat it before he…!

(FANGS grabs HONOR.)

FANGS: Bubble gum's not gonna save you from my fangs!

(FANGS prepares to bite HONOR's neck.)

MISS BLYTON: Honor, breathe it in his face! Full in his face!

(HONOR does so. Instantly FANGS recoils away from HONOR in horror.)

FANGS: UGHHH! She's breathed garlic right up me 'ooter! An' garlic's the Curse of Vampires. 'S'orrible! 'S'worse than Winny's cookin'!

(HONOR hugs MISS BLYTON.)

HONOR: Oh you're so with it, Miss Blyton, so with it!

MISS BLYTON: *(Bowing.)* Thank you, my dear. And now you've both learnt a much-needed lesson, let's high-tail out of this graveyard before things really get rough. Then I will return in the morning alone, and sort everything out.

FANGS: No, the kids can't leave now. I've got to 'ave a couple of pints of their blood first!

(FANGS charges at the CHILDREN, but CLIVE is too quick for him. With his wizard's staff, CLIVE trips FANGS up. This time FANGS falls into an open grave – down through the stage trap.)

HONOR: I do hope he hasn't hurt himself too much.

MISS BLYTON: He's fine, dear. You must remember that the inside of a dank grave is the nearest thing to home for a vampire.

FANGS: *(Bellowing from the depths of the grave.)* 'Ey, you lot, 'elp me outta 'ere! It's 'orrbly smelly down 'ere. And ruddy muddy! So, someone, gimme a hand!

(FANGS' hand appears over the edge of the grave.)

MISS BLYTON: Certainly not. *(She gives FANGS a school-marm's slap on the back of his wrist.)* You've been a very bad bat! Now come along, children.

FANGS: *(From the depths of the grave.)* Please, you've gotta let me outta 'ere! Before I 'ave a vampire's nervous breakdown! Oh snot, spit and bogies! Now see what you've done to me? Me teeth've dropped out. And I can't find 'em under all this blasted mud.

HONOR: Well, now poor Fangs has lost his fangs, surely he can't do us any harm? So can't we help him out of the grave?

MISS BLYTON: No. *(To FANGS.)* Until you tell us everything you know about Sir Lucifer's evil plans, I will only allow you to poke your head above the grave.

(In response, only FANGS' head and shoulders emerge from the grave.)

FANGS: I'll tell you everything, everything. *(He points to his open mouth.)* 'Cause you're right; I'm such a failure. I'm the first vampire, who's ever lost 'is fangs. So I'm not even a write-off, I'm a total *bite*-off. Get it? I'm not a write-off. *(Demonstrating.)* I'm a total bite-off!

CLIVE: You sure are, mate. See, wot you need is to watch a re-run of 'Buffy the Vampire Slayer', and then you'd pick up a few hints on how a *real* vampire behaves. 'Cause at the moment you're just an all-time loser.

FANGS: *(Starting to cry.)* I know, I know. You don't 'ave to tell me. *(Blubbering.)* I fink it's 'cause me 'eart aint in it. You see, I really hate bein' 'orrible, but I can't stop meself – 'cause I'm under the control of… the control of…

(FANGS' blubbering is cut short by the piercing sound of an eerie whistle that emanates from the darkness, accompanied by an ominous drumbeat. In response FANGS freezes.)

MISS BLYTON: Oh botheration! Just as Fangs was about to spill the beans, Sir Lucifer's put another of his devilish spells on him!

(As the whistle and drumbeat intensify, FANGS produces another set of fangs from his pocket. Then ceremonially he inserts them into his mouth.)

FANGS: *(As if in a trance.)* Yes, Master. At once, Master. I'll choke on their blood, and then I'll suck their skins dry.

(Then…before the CHILDREN's horrified eyes, FANGS rises out of the misty grave – as if by magic. Now he towers above them because he has become the terrifying Count Dracula.

MISS BLYTON and the CHILDREN cower.

There is an iridescent flash of lightning, followed by crashing thunder. FANGS opens his black cloak like the wings of a gigantic bat.)

MISS BLYTON: Now stay right where you are, Fangs, like a good bat.

FANGS: Silence, human! You are now in *my* realm; the Kingdom of the Undead. *(FANGS beckons to HONOR.)* Come here, child; I wish to drink your life-blood. *(With and imperious gesture.)* No, Blyton, do not try to move, or speak – because you cannot prevent this. I am the son of Count Dracula. So, when the foul sun sinks into my grave, I arise, like the true vampire I am. Then I gallop through the stifling dark in my midnight coach, making all the children shudder in their beds. And each of them wonders who will be my next victim, to be transformed into a vampire like myself. Well, they need wonder no longer – because I choose you…Honor. (*MISS BLYTON and CLIVE remain frozen under FANGS' spell, and they can do nothing as HONOR, who appears to be sleep-walking, continues to move towards the beckoning FANGS.)* Unbutton your collar, child. My fangs hunger to sink into your soft skin. Then your clear, red blood will gush into my throat – because now…you are mine…and soon you, too, will be dead, yet living, as *I* am. (*He is about to sink his fangs into HONOR's neck when…BRUNO roars into view, beating his chest like a gorilla! FANGS holds HONOR with one arms, and he points his outstretched claw at BRUNO.)* Too late, Bruno! No one can prevent me drinking my fill of this girl's blood! NO ONE!

(Strobe lighting illuminates the COMBATANTS as the Fight Music begins. Then BRUNO and FANGS start their strobe-lit, slow-motion Battle for supremacy. First one, and then the other, gains advantage. The CHILDREN and MISS BLYTON remain frozen, because they are under FANGS' spell.

Then, finally, BRUNO gains the upper hand in the Battle.)

BRUNO: Here, take this, you ragbag rat-bat!

(With his huge paw, BRUNO knocks FANGS out. Then BRUNO claps his paws together, and the Fight Music stops abruptly. Simultaneously the Stage Lightning returns to normal – as the CHILDREN and MISS BLYTON are released from FANGS' spell. Then HONOR hugs BRUNO.)

HONOR: Oh thank you, Mr Bruno, thank you for saving me!

MISS BLYTON: It was certainly time someone did something useful.

CLIVE: *(To BRUNO.)* Yeah, an' where the hell did you disappear to, anyway?

BRUNO: That wasn't my intention. I wanted to come straight back to you, but, you see, Sir Lucifer…Sir Luci…

(But BRUNO is cut short by a prolonged sinister whistling-sound, accompanied by a hypnotic drumbeat – as the darkness engulfs the CHILDREN and MISS BLYTON. Instantly BRUNO is thrown into a trance.

Then, to the CHILDREN's surprise, BRUNO slings the unconscious FANGS over his shoulder, and like an automaton, BRUNO exits with his burden.)

MISS BLYTON: *(To the CHILDREN, about BRUNO and FANGS.)* They're mad! They're both stark-staring mad!

HONOR: *(Still somewhat frightened.)* Yes, you're right, Miss Blyton. In fact it seems that you've been right all along.

CLIVE: Yeah, we're very sorry we didn't trust you in the first place, Miss B.

HONOR: *(To MISS BLYTON.)* So what you think we should now, then?

MISS BLYTON: We must get out of here immediately, and then we must call the Police because they are our only hope now.

CLIVE: Yeah, but I thought you said that you could sort Sir Lucifer an' 'is gang out all on yer own?

MISS BLYTON: I did. But I was wrong. Very wrong. So now let's get out of here before it's too late.

(But as they move to go, there is a sudden burst of ear-shattering music. Then before MISS BLYTON and the CHILDREN can escape, WINNY as a beautiful but evil-looking witch, and FANGS as Dracula,

and BRUNO as King Kong, dance wildly into view, from opposite sides of the graveyard. They are singing a macabre Rock Number.)

ROCK NUMBER: **It's rock, rock, rock,**
on Hallowe'en night!
It's shock, shock, shock!
We'll give you a fright.
'Cause we're as evil, as evil can be!
Even Evil Knevil's not as evil as we!
So we'll rock, and we'll roll,
and we'll gobble…gobble you whole;
'cause the Dead have arisen,
and so have we!
And we mean to have you kids for tea!

(MISS BLYTON tries to attack the demonic DANCERS, but they soon overpower her, and they tie her up in her Manchester United scarf.)

ROCK SONG: **Yes, it's rock, rock, rock!**
She's tied up in her scarf.
It's shock, shock, shock!
We'll cut you in half!
'Cause we're as hungry, as hungry can be!
Suck your blood for dinner, scrunch your bones for tea!
We'll skive, and we'll jive,
with the Devil's scythe, the Devil's scythe!
For the Dead have risen,
and so have we!
And we mean to have you kids for tea!

(During the Rock Number, the Carousel spins around to reveal – a huge, strobe-lit Mask of the Devil.

Lightning and thunder is accompanied by a stereophonic fanfare of trumpets.

EVERYONE freezes. Enter SIR LUCIFER, smiling.)

SIR LUCIFER: Welcome, minions – to Hallowe'en, which is my greatest Sabbat. Lucifer bids you welcome.

(LIGHTS dim; until only SIR LUCIFER can be seen. With a Satanic flourish, he removes his topper to reveal…his Devil's Horns! Then, even more elaborately, SIR LUCIFER unzips his left trouser leg, and he pulls out…his Forked Tail. Then he waves his Cloven Hoof.

A flash of lightning. Instant BLACKOUT.

Almost as quickly, the LIGHTS return.

Then again the Rock Music throbs into life. Like three gyrating demons, FANGS, WINNY and BRUNO whirl MISS BLYTON around, as their dancing becomes wilder and wilder. Even the CHILDREN are sucked into the Dance.)

ROCK SONG: **It's rock, rock, rock!**
In Lucifer's name!
It's shock, shock, shock!
Hell-Fire and pain!
'Cause we're as happy, as happy can be
that the Devil controls our destiny!
And we'll rock, and we'll roll
like the Dragon and the Troll.
A Rock'n'Roll Troll!
So turn right around, take a look and see
that Hell is here for Eternity!
Hell is here for Eternity!
Hell is here for Eternity.
HELL IS HERE…!

(Thunder. The Carousel turns to reveal LUCIFER, in all his Satanic glory, as he sits on his Dark Throne, holding his Devil's Trident.

Instantly WINNY, FANGS and BRUNO cower to their knees before their Satanic MASTER singing.)

WINNY: **All Hail, Great Lucifer! King Satan!**

FANGS: **All Hail, Lord of the Flies!**

BRUNO: **All Hail, Master of the World!**

FANGS/WINNY/BRUNO: *(Shouting in unison.)* HAIL! HAIL! HAIL!

(LUCIFER points his Devil's Trident at the still semi-defiant CHILDREN.)

LUCIFER: Kneel, humans, in the presence of the Emperor of Hell!

HONOR: Never!

CLIVE: An' I'm not goin' to, neither!

LUCIFER: Then lose your gift of Speech! There is no point in trying to answer back. You cannot. And if you dare to defy me further, I will freeze up your blood and jellify your bones! *(Laughing.)* You are such stupid children to have the mindless arrogance and foolish courage to attend my Hallowe'en Party, when this night is my greatest Festival of Evil Darkness. *(To HONOR.)* And you truly thought that I would give you money, girl, to help your miserable Mother? *(To CLIVE.)* Or that I would help you, boy, gain your freedom from the orphanage, and buy you some unnecessary parents? How gullible you children are! Because – instead of helping either of you! – I intend to destroy your mother, girl! And as for you, boy – I will send you back to your orphanage with a broken mind and heart. And I can do all this because I am the Ruler of the World! And tonight I will open all the graveyards, so that the Dead – so many, many Dead – can break into the houses, seize all the Children. Then the dead will take possession of the Earth forever! *(To WINNY, FANGS and BRUNO.)* Slaves! Escort the Humans into the Halls of Hell, and then do exactly as I commanded you.

(Crash of thunder. The CHILDREN are carried off by BRUNO and FANGS, with WINNY in attendance.)

LUCIFER: Now I will complete my final preparation for the Children's eternal doom.

(Thunder. The Carousel swings round, leaving us with the Devil's strobe-lit Mask.

Light pinpoints MISS BLYTON, struggling to free herself from being bound by her Manchester United scarf.)

MISS BLYTON: *(To the Audience.)* I'd better vamoose, and get some help!

(MISS BLYTON runs off. Simultaneously there is the triumphant cackle of WINNY the Witch's laughter. Then we hear MISS BLYTON scream!

BLACKOUT.)

SCENE TWO

LIGHTS come up on the Carousel in the graveyard.

WINNY, who is now dressed like a Black Cat, and FANGS, who is a Black Bat, and BRUNO, who is King Kong, step off the Carousel, and they sing to the Audience, with BRUNO beginning the song.

BRUNO: **O listen to us, for the End is near.
The Children are changed beyond compare.**

WINNY: **The Children are changed, and filled with fear.**

FANGS: **They've become like Us, and must despair!**

BRUNO: **And I warned them both to 'Beware! Beware'
of our Master, the Devil, and not to come back!
Yes, I warned the Children to take good care.
But they didn't listen. The outlook's Black!**

FANGS: **He'll turn them now into something rare.**

WINNY: **They'll be changed like me to…a Witch's Cat!**

BRUNO: **Or changed like me to…a King Kong Bear!**

FANGS: **Or changed like me to…a Vampire Bat!**

(There is a thunderous roll on the timpani.

The Carousel moves round to reveal a Punch-and-Judy stand; and the CHILDREN have been turned into Puppets! They have strings attached to their wrists, elbows, knees and ankles, and they are being made to dance like puppets. And LUCIFER is sitting on top of the Carousel, pulling the CHILDREN's strings, and manipulating them. As he does so, LUCIFER sings.)

LUCIFER: **But I have changed them
into even worse things!
I have changed them to Puppets!
And I am pulling the strings!**

(The sight of the CHILDREN dancing like puppets is grotesque, but also it is very moving. Then mechanically, WINNY, FANGS and BRUNO throw balls at the CHILDREN as if they were skittles.

The CHILDREN start to sing of their despair.)

HONOR: **O please...free us!**

CLIVE: **Please...let us go!**

HONOR: **Please...believe us...**

CLIVE: **...We...didn't know...**

TOGETHER: **...of the terrors of magic on Lucifer's Night.
Can't you see what you're doing just isn't right?
Please, let's go home while the moon is still bright.
While the moon...is still bright.
So please... free us!
Please...let us go!
Please...believe us...
We.......didn't know
the Horrors of Witchcraft are as real as the Night.
Can't you see what you're doing just isn't right?
Please, let's go home while the moon...is still bright.
While the moon...is still bright.**

(Heavy Rock Music takes over. WINNY, FANGS and BRUNO dance around the CHILDREN while LUCIFER sings.)

LUCIFER'S SONG: **Too late, too late, you're much too late!**

I hate, I have, I have too much hate
to make you free, to let you go!
I need, you see, to bake you as dough.
So keep on dancing the Dance of Despair,
'cause tomorrow I'm telling you,
tomorrow I'm selling you
at Lucifer's Fair!
Yes, keep on dancing the Dance of Despair,
'cause tomorrow I'm telling you,
tomorrow I'm selling you
at Lucifer's Fair!

(At that moment a COCKEREL crows in the distance. LUCIFER looks terrified.)

LUCIFER: No, not yet!

HONOR: *(To CLIVE.)* It's the dawn!

CLIVE: Oh look, Honor! Look at the sun!

(The sky begins to turn pink.)

HONOR: Beautiful…the sky is so beautiful.

(As the first rays of the morning sunlight illuminate the CHILDREN, they begin to sing.)

CHILDREN'S SONG: **O please… free us!**
Please…let us go!
You must…believe us
that's the first….cockcrow.
The Terrors of Magic are over and done.
All the world's singing; 'Here comes the sun.'
Your power is broken, and now we have won.
We have won! WE HAVE WON!

LUCIFER: *(Shouting.)* Never!

(The music fades into…the sounds of the Dawn Chorus.)

WINNY: It's the Dawn Chorus!

LUCIFER: *(Waving his Devil's Trident.)* Rubbish! It's just a lot of stupid birds sounding off like an alarm clock to wake up the rest of this pathetic world.

WINNY: No, it's far more than that. Because I'm fed up with being a witch. I want to be a gym mistress again, waving my jolly old hockey stick.

FANGS: Yes, I wanna be just an old fashioned Rocker again.

LUCIFER: Impossible! You're all my slaves forever and ever!

(BRUNO waves his paws at LUCIFER.)

BRUNO: No! I'm sick of all this shaggy hair, and these ridiculous paws. I want to be a Man again. I want to be Free! I want to be me!

LUCIFER: Enough of this madness! You can never be Free. You'll always be a King Kong animal for the rest of your life. Terrorising children, smashing down houses, and pulling planes out of the sky!

(BRUNO slumps down onto his knees in front of LUCIFER and sings.)

BRUNO: **O Please...free me!**
Please...let me go!

(WINNY goes down on her knees beside BRUNO, and imploringly she sings to LUCIFER.)

WINNY: **Yes, please........free us!**
Please............let us go!

BRUNO: **You must........believe us**
that is the first........cockcrow.

(The music continues.)

FANGS: *(Speaking.)* They're right, Boss. You can't 'old us against our wills anymore. I'm fed-up wiv bein' 'orrible. These fangs give me jaw-ache, blood gives me indigestion, I keep losin' me wings, an' I can't fly anyway.

LUCIFER: Silence, Bat Ears!

(The Lights turn Crimson.

LUCIFER conjures a microphone out of the air, and bursts into song.)

LUCIFER'S SONG: **Whatever you say,**
however you pray,
you'll be a Vampire Bat 'till Judgement Day!
You'll fly over moats.
You'll rip necks and throats!
Suck blood, and eat skin
through thick and thin.

(HONOR and CLIVE have had as much as they can take, and to LUCIFER's horrified surprise, they sing their defiance.)

CHILDREN'S SONG: **No, he won't! Blood-sucking's a sin!**
And now it's time for Us Children to win!
From this point on,
neither money nor gain
can make us do wrong,
or put us to shame!

When Two become One, and share all their pain,
Together they triumph, and the Devil is slain!
Together they're crowned as the Queen and the
King!
Their fear disappears, and the morning larks sing;
and their hands tear off the Devil's Wings,
and together they break!...break!...break!...
Together they break!...
THEIR PUPPET STRINGS!

(There is the sound of strings snapping!

Then, to everyone's amazement, they see that the CHILDREN have broken their puppet strings, and now the CHILDREN stand free.)

WINNY: Gym-slips and hockey-sticks!
They're free! They're free!

FANGS: Snake's-hips and dirty tricks!
    They free! They're free!

CHILDREN: And by the time we're finished, so will *you* be!

LUCIFER: No, they can never leave my Kingdom 'till Eternity!

(HONOR and CLIVE address FANGS, WINNY and BRUNO.)

HONOR: Friends; take each other's hands.

CLIVE: Form a circle…

HONOR: …And SEE!

FANGS: We can't!

WINNY: We daren't!

BRUNO: Because we'll never be free!

HONOR: You can…

CLIVE: …and you must!

LUCIFER: If you do as they say, I'll turn you to dust!

HONOR: Take notice of him…

CLIVE: ….and close your eyes.

(Nervously WINNY, FANGS and BRUNO do as the CHILDREN tell them.)

HONOR: Now listen to your hearts…

CLIVE: …and think of the sunrise.

LUCIFER: Stop this, stop this! And obey the Lord of Flies!

HONOR: No, believe in Goodness and Love…

CLIVE: …and the Bat will change into a Dove…

HONOR: …the Witch's Broomstick to a Rainbow Fan…

BRUNO: …and the King Kong Bear to a Gentle Man.

HONOR: Yes, and Love will give you the Strength and the
Power…

CLIVE: …to change back to *Yourselves* in the Rising Sun.

HONOR: And your Faith will open your Hearts like a Flower.

CLIVE: So believe in the Truth, and Lucifer's done!

HONOR: Then you will be Human again…

CLIVE: …and suffer no more Witchcraft Pain!

HONOR: One moment more!…

CLIVE: …and only one!

(The COCKEREL crows again triumphantly.)

CHILDREN: And now, my friends, you have won! YOU
HAVE WON!

*(There is a pause. Then WINNY, FANGS and BRUNO advance on
the now-frightened figure of LUCIFER, who is now cowering on top
of the Carousel.)*

LUCIFER: *(Stuttering.)* Wh-what are you all l-looking at m-me
like that f-for?

FANGS: Sorry, Boss, but I'm afraid we're revoltin'!

LUCIFER: You most certainly are! In fact you're the most
'revolting' reptiles I've clapped my eyes on.

BRUNO: Down with Lucifer!

*(With a great roar, BRUNO pulls LUCIFER off the Carousel. Then
he chases him around the graveyard. Immediately CLIVE and
HONOR go into their 'Plan'; i.e., HONOR kneels, and makes a back,
while CLIVE prods LUCIFER's bum with the Devil's Trident. Then
LUCIFER trips over the kneeling HONOR. With an anguished cry,
LUCIFER disappears into the open grave.)*

LUCIFER: *(From the depths of the grave.)* Get me out of here! It's
hellish cold. I'll catch my death!

(FANGS rushes forward.)

FANGS: One, two, three! Orf wiv his 'orns!

(There is a brief flurry as FANGS pulls off LUCIFER's horns.)

LUCIFER: Oh moles, trolls and burning coals!

(Then BRUNO, FANGS and WINNY pull LUCIFER out of the grave.)

WINNY: Now off with his forked tail!

(BRUNO sits on LUCIFER while WINNY pulls off his forked tail. She throws the tail to CLIVE, who cracks it like a whip.)

CLIVE: Makes a wicked bullwhip!

(CLIVE bonks LUCIFER with the 'whip'.)

LUCIFER: OUUCH! Give me my tail back!

(BRUNO slams his foot on LUCIFER's chest. Then he levels LUCIFER's forked trident at LUCIFER's throat.)

BRUNO: Now confess your sins, Lucy, or I'll rip out your Adam's apple!

LUCIFER: *(Jibbering with fear.)* Alright, alright, I admit that I'm not really the Devil at all. 'Fact during the day, I'm just a nasty, crooked landlord. And at night, I go in for some even nastier Black Magic. Yes, and the only reason I've been able to control you all is because I'm rather good at hypnotising people. Particularly dumb-dumbs like you three.

(Enter MISS BLYTON, dressed as Sherlock Holmes, complete with his pipe and magnifying glass.)

MISS BLYTON: Well, as I am Sherlock Holmes, I'm going to take you to Court with all the incriminating evidence I've gathered against you.

LUCIFER: You've got no proof to have me locked up, you amateur. See, I take back everything I said.

(*MISS BLYTON produces a pocket-recorder.*)

MISS BLYTON: Too late, mate,
'cause now I've got you on tape, you ape. (*Playing the recorder to LUCIFER.*) 'During the day I'm just a nasty, crooked landlord. And at night, I go in for some nastier Black Magic...'

LUCIFER: You sneaky, stinking Sherlock!

MISS BLYTON: It was elementary, my dear Moriarty.

LUCIFER: Well, if I'm to be destroyed, Winny and Fangs are going to come down with me! 'Cause I can prove that our Gym Mistress here has been practising Black Magic, too. As for Fangs, he's broken his parole.
So if you throw me in the can, Miss B,
these two suckers are going to end up beside me.
So, as usual, you are trapped in Lucifer's Wood,
and, once again, Evil triumphs over good!

BRUNO: (*Roaring.*) No, no, *I* will testify on behalf of Fangs and Winny!

LUCIFER: (*Roaring with laughter.*) You?! That's the biggest laugh of the century!

(*Suddenly BRUNO goes into convulsions. The OTHERS surround BRUNO, masking him from the AUDIENCE. As they draw back from BRUNO's apparently lifeless body...the POLICEMAN, from the First Scene of the Play, steps out of BRUNO's bear skin!*

Then the POLICEMAN advances on LUCIFER with a pair of handcuffs.)

LUCIFER: What the devil d'you think you're doing, Bruno?

(*The POLICEMAN handcuffs LUCIFER.*)

P.C. BRUNO: I'm arrestin' you in the name of the Law, Lucy. That's wot I'm doin'.

LUCIFER: O my Mars Bar and Gobstopper!
I forgot you were originally a copper!

P.C. BRUNO: *(Saluting.)* Yes, it's P.C. Bruno, at your service, ladies and gentlemen.

HONOR: Amazing. You look just like the policeman that questioned me this morning.

P.C. BRUNO: I *am* the policeman who questioned you this mornin'. But when I left you, I nipped over the fence to inspect this 'ere Fair that never seemed to open. Unfortunately before I could take any action and call for back-up… *(Pointing to LUCIFER.)* …this vicious old Satanist 'ere tripped me up with his trident. Then he had the perishin' nerve to hypnotise me into believin' that I was just a clapped-out, giant teddy bear!

CLIVE: Stroll on.

P.C. BRUNO: You can say that again. Well, thanks, folks, for all your help. But now, if you don't mind, I'll take this nasty piece of work back to one our local cells.

LUCIFER: *(Laughing derisively.)* Please do. And the moment we arrive, Officer, I will give instructions for this girl's mother's home to be demolished.

HONOR: Oh Sir Lucifer, please, I beg you…

MISS BLYTON: *(Interrupting.)* Oh don't worry, my dear. He has no power to do any such thing, because I shall ensure that the Council charges Lucy with all his corrupt practices.

(HONOR hugs MISS BLYTON.)

HONOR: Oh Miss B, you are so clever!

MISS BLYTON: And, furthermore, if your mother agrees, I'm coming to live with you, so I can thwart any other diabolical plans that Lucy may concoct in the future.

HONOR: How can you possibly come and live with us, Miss Blyton?

MISS BLYTON: Because I'm your long-lost Aunty Enid from America, dear.

HONOR: Good Heavens.

LUCIFER: Ugh! How revoltingly sloppy can you get. Still, at least I'll be revenged on Clive. *(To CLIVE.)* Because I'll report your whereabouts to St Joseph's. Then they'll come and fetch you, and they'll never let you out again!

MISS BLYTON: Again you're wrong, Lucy. You see, Clive is coming to live at my sisters with Honor and me.

CLIVE: Wot?!

MISS BLYTON: And if you're willing, Clive, I would like to try to adopt you – as my son.

CLIVE: Blimey. But I suppose 'avin' Wonder Woman, Florence Nightingale an' Sherlock 'Olmes as my mother won't be too bad.

LUCIFER: Ugh! It gets sloppier and sloppier. If only I were a real Devil, I would…

WINNY: Fortunately you're not a real Devil, sweetie-pie…

FANGS: …So you're off to prison to have a good cry!

LUCIFER: Alright, alright. I'm off to jail!
But somehow yet I will make things worse.
Before I've finished, you'll all turn pale.
Until then, I leave you – with LUCIFER'S CURSE!

(P.C. BRUNO is about to take LUCIFER to jail when MISS BLYTON addresses him.)

MISS BLYTON: Officer.

P.C. BRUNO: Yes, Miss Blyton.

MISS BLYTON: Do come to our house, 18 Leconfrost Avenue, tonight because we're having a *real* Party.

P.C. BRUNO: Oh thank you, I will. Well, mornin', all. Come on, Lucy.

(P.C. BRUNO and LUCIFER exit.)

MISS BLYTON: Now, my dears, we're all happy at last;
    so let's dance home, and have some break…fast.

*(The CHILDREN groan at MISS BLYTON's appalling rhyme. Then
the Stage darkens.*

*HONOR walks into the Centre Spot and begins to sing to the
Audience.)*

HONOR: **Let's dance home through the autumn leaves.**
    We're free from the dark, and Sir Lucifer's Fair.
    Let's dance under the golden trees.
    Gone are the Vampire, the Witch and the Bear.
    See the frost thaw on the hard earth.
    Let's dance, let's dance, let's dance for all we are
    worth.

    See the Sun shining, and see the mist rise.
    Life is so rich, and childhood sweet;
    round every corner's a sunshine surprise.
    Let's dance through the wood and down to the street.
    We'll sing to the world of the sky and the sea.
    The nightmare is over, and now we are free!

*(The Stage is ablaze with light as EVERYONE sings and dances
ecstatically.)*

CHORUS: **Let's dance home through the autumn leaves.**
    We're free from the dark and Sir Lucifer's Fair.
    Let's dance under the golden trees.
    Gone are the Vampire, the Witch and the Bear.
    See the frost thaw on the hard earth.
    Let's dance, let's dance, let's dance for all we are
    worth.

CHORUS: **'Bye, 'bye, Lucifer. 'Bye, 'bye, Lucifer.**
    Lock him up down under, and make it double quick!
    'Bye, 'bye, Lucifer. 'Bye, 'bye, Lucifer.
    The Devil's off to Strangeways, Old Nick is in the
    nick.
    'Bye, 'bye, Lucifer. 'Bye, 'bye, Lucifer!

Your game is up. No one else will play.
Bye, 'bye, Lucifer. 'Bye, 'bye, Lucifer.
All evil Powers of Darkness have faded with the day!

'Bye, 'bye, Lucifer. 'Bye, 'bye, Lucifer.
Lock him up down under, and make it double quick!
'Bye, 'bye, Lucifer. 'Bye, 'bye, Lucifer.
The Devil's off to Strangeways, Old Nick is in the
nick.
'Bye, 'bye, Lucifer. 'Bye, 'bye, Lucifer!
Lock him up down under, and make it double quick!
Bye, 'bye, Lucifer. 'Bye, 'bye, Lucifer!
The Devil's off to Strangeways, Old Nick is in the
nick.
Lock him up down under, and make it double quick!

*(There is a fanfare of trumpets. 'LUCIFER'S FAIR' is illuminated
in neon lights on the Carousel, and the stage glows with autumnal
colours.*

*As they all dance together, the CHILDREN's verse and the CHORUS
are now sung in counterpoint…until the two melodies join.)*

CHORUS: **Let's dance home through the autumn leaves.
We're free from the dark and Sir Lucifer's Fair.
Let's dance under the golden trees.
Gone are the Vampire, the Witch and the Bear.
See the Sun shining, and see the mist rise.
Life is so rich, and childhood sweet;
round every corner's a sunshine surprise.
Let's dance through the wood and down to the street.
We'll sing to the world of the sky and the sea.
The nightmare is over, and now…we are free!
WE ARE FREE! WE ARE FREE! WE ARE FREE!**

*(The ENSEMBLE Song-and-Dance routine finishes in joyful ebullience
and the CAST gaze into the Audience, radiant and triumphant.*

Blackout.)

THE END